*To my mother, Kathryn Weeks, who taught me that attention to small details brings beauty and festivity to the occasions of life.*

*Kathy Peel*

*To my mother, Trula Casey, who exemplified the joy of homemaking and taught me to realize the high calling of motherhood.*

*Judie Byrd*

# Table of Contents

## Acknowledgments

Many people have helped us with this book in countless ways:

Our faithful friends at Focus on the Family: Chuck Bolte, Jon Killingsworth, Dean Merrill, Bev Rykerd, Nancy Wallace and Rolf Zettersten, who have shared our dreams of helping families have fun together and who have worked tirelessly behind the scenes; Sheila Cragg and Janet Kobobel, our editors, who have patiently helped us solidify our dreams in black and white.

Dr. James Dobson, whose dream of strengthening the American family has been an inspiration to us and has provided us with guidance, resources and encouragement in raising our own families.

Our wonderful husbands, who give us support, freedom and a lot of flexibility to pursue our dreams.

Our incredible children, who dream with us, cheer us on, taste-test our receipes and make our crafts.

Our dear friend and project-partner Dan Johnson, who is the most creative person and biggest dreamer we know.

The following friends, who have shared their expertise, holiday ideas and traditions with us: Debby Brown, Ann Butler, Natalie Chovolla, Olivia Eudaly, Boyd Griffith, Emma John Helm, Gwen Hoffman, Judy Holze, Jan Jenison, Pat Lindgren, Jan Luskey, Sylvia Luskey, Ann Magoffin, Joy Mahaffey, Mindy Page, Carol Stripling, Jodi Tjoelker, Julia Watts, Amy Yahnig and Peggy Zadina.

# Introduction

What does the word *holiday* mean to your family? Do your children think the smoke alarm goes off automatically when their birthday cakes are done? Does the bank's overdraft department put your telephone number on its automatic-speed-dial list at Christmastime? Do you overdose on antacids just thinking about playing hostess for the neighborhood Fourth of July picnic?

**"Holidays are the exclamation points of life!"**

The thought of planning a celebration may terrify or tire you; yet it's those special occasions that bring family and friends together. Holidays are times when we can laugh, love and enjoy life. And those are three things we need large doses of regularly!

In *A Mother's Manual for Holiday Survival*, we've included an entire year's supply of celebrations to help your family transform mundane moments into magnificent memories. When you feel exhausted and out of ideas, this catalog of creative resources will inspire and stimulate your imagination. On the days when you are short on time, patience and money, you'll find easy, inexpensive activities to keep your kids entertained and out of mischief. Easy-to-follow tips and techniques will help you carry on old traditions and establish new ones.

As you think about planning special occasions and celebrating holidays, remember that the object is to have fun and make positive memories. Part of the fun is being able to laugh with your family about your own flops.

Judie's kids still snicker about the time she caught her oven on fire cooking baked Alaska. And Kathy's family won't let her forget about the molded gelatin salad she took to a Fourth of July picnic. The 100-degree heat turned her masterpiece into a soupy mess.

Accept the fact that calamity and confusion are often uninvited guests at family celebrations. Do yourself and your family a favor by finding humor in those inevitable mishaps that plague us all. Don't expect heaven on earth!

Only in heaven will:

—it never rain on the day of your picnic.

—you always remember to buy film for your camera before the special occasion.

—your cakes always come out of the pan in one piece.

—the birthday punch not produce a flypaper effect when spilled on your freshly mopped floor.

—you always be prepared for unexpected guests who give your bookshelves the white-glove treatment.

—the kids want to mow the lawn instead of watch TV on the day of your party.

—your children compete to see who gets to do the dishes after the party.

—you smile when the family reunion at the beach is over and your only memento is a suitcase filled with mildewed swimsuits.

—you not hear any complaints about eating turkey sandwiches, turkey potpie and turkey tetrazzini the week after Thanksgiving.

—you be able to smile and say thank you without guilt on Christmas Day when you receive one more plaster-of-paris handprint instead of jewelry.

We hope our book will help you seize new opportunities to celebrate holidays, special occasions and every other day of the year!

*Kathy Peel*
*Judie Byrd*

# Chapter 1

# Great Ways to Add Fun to Any Holiday

"I remember, I remember,
When the holiday was done,
Just sittin' around the table
And talkin' about the fun."

"Let's think of a way to tease Daddy when he comes home from work. I'll bet he forgot it's April Fools' Day!"

"Why do we always go to the cemetery to put a flag on Uncle Ed's grave on Memorial Day?"

"Mommy, I saw pumpkins at a roadside stand today. When can we get ours?"

Holidays are especially significant to children. Their playful minds rarely miss an opportunity to celebrate. Anticipating the occasion can be as much fun for them as the holiday itself. A child's mind is also a curator of memories. Taking a little extra time to create family celebrations will build a rich museum of positive remembrances for your family.

Moreover, special traditions and rituals promote family bonding. There's just something about being able to say "This is the way we always do it" that cements a family together.

Although most of us want to create opportunities for our families to celebrate, we can't bear the thought of adding one more thing to our schedules. If we're caught off guard when a holiday rolls around, we often become frustrated and feel guilty because we weren't prepared.

To help you keep track of the holidays and special occasions, we've included a list of holidays and two helpful planners following this chapter. The first is a Holiday and Special Occasion Planner for organizing a party or special event. Duplicate the blank chart, and use it to make your plans. When the celebration is over, make a few remarks on the back of it about what worked well and what you would do differently. Then file it for reference when you plan future parties.

The second chart is the Celebration Planning Calendar for recording anniversaries, birthdays, holidays and other special days. We've included a place to write the date, the holiday or occasion and your plans or activity for that event. It may be as simple as noting that you need to send a greeting card, buy or make a gift or plan a picnic.

Make copies of the blank calendar to fill in. Be sure to add a few surprise ways to make ordinary days fun. You'll find ideas in chapter 13, "75 Ways to Celebrate Every Day," and in chapter 14, "Celebrating on a Shoestring." At the beginning of each year, make a new calendar. Put in gift ideas ahead of time; then watch for sales. You might want to file these charts or keep them in a notebook for reference in years to come.

For those special occasions, here are some simple ideas you can pull out of the hat to make a memory no matter what holiday you're celebrating.

## Quick and Easy Ways to Celebrate Any Holiday

1. Add pizzazz to your meals when you celebrate. You don't have to fix an elaborate meal; just a few extra touches will make an ordinary breakfast, lunch or dinner a special occasion. For example, serve different kinds of red foods on Valentine's Day. Decorate each plate with edible flowers such as pansies or daisy petals on the first day of spring. You can also purchase a plate that says: "You Are Special Today." This plate comes in handy when you want to honor a family member or friend at a meal.

2. Keep various colors of balloons, candles, confetti and crepe-paper streamers for spur-of-the-moment celebrations. It takes only a few minutes to create a festive atmosphere.

3. Make paper-doll-style garlands to string across windows or doors. Kids love to make garlands of yellow tulips; red, white and blue stars; or brown gingerbread people.

4. Create an easy, festive centerpiece. Your kids will love helping you make a new one for each season. Use a clear-glass hurricane shade 12 inches tall and 4½ inches in diameter. (This shade is also a candle lantern and is available at craft stores.) Place the shade in the center of your table. If you want a base for the shade, use a clear-glass plate or a tray. Fill the shade with various seasonal items. For example, use alternating layers of pastel eggs and Spanish moss for Easter. In the fall, fill the shade with tiny pumpkins, acorns and pecans, tying a raffia bow around the outside of the glass. At Christmas, fill it with crabapples or a collection of old Christmas balls.

5. Design wreaths or door decorations for different holidays and seasons. One mom has a job that requires her to travel. As an easy way to make her home festive, she puts a different decoration on the front door the first day of each month. These decorations do not need to be elaborate but can be fun and inexpensive. You can put up a "Happy New Year" banner on January 1, a spring wreath with flowers and rabbits on April 1 or a cardboard Uncle Sam poster on July 1.

6. Keep greeting cards, different-colored note paper and pens, festive stickers and stamps on hand. Send a special message to someone for a holiday greeting. Grandparents love to receive cards from grandkids. Kathy enjoys sending humorous cards to friends on April Fools' Day.

7. Phone family members and friends. Don't wait for their birthdays or Christmas. Call just to say, "Happy first day of summer" or "Happy Veterans Day."

**Creative Cakes for Any Celebration**

8. Make festive cakes or cupcakes with your kids. Keep a cake mix, can of frosting and food coloring in the pantry. It's fun to bake different-colored holiday cakes, such as green for St. Patrick's Day or orange for Halloween. Use a white cake mix, simply substituting up to 1 ounce of food coloring (depending on the desired intensity of the color) for 1 ounce of liquid called for in the recipe. Then add drops of food coloring to white frosting until you have the desired color.

9. Keep decorating items on hand, such as chocolate chips, colored sprinkles, red-hots and silver dragées. You can also use maraschino cherries, chocolate candies, colored coconut, gumdrops, nuts and raisins.

10. Create fun cakes with small plastic toys and animals. (Party supply stores carry decorating items.) To create landscapes, use chocolate frosting to ice the cake; drop spoonfuls of icing on top and form them into hills and valleys. Use tinted-green coconut for grass and crushed chocolate wafers for dirt.

11. Make a race-car cake with strings of licorice for the track and small plastic cars.

12. Form a trail of small plastic ants crawling on the cake for a picnic or for a fun after-school surprise.

13. Use fresh flowers (make sure they aren't poisonous) to make an especially pretty cake.

Carnations, geraniums, marigolds, pansies, roses and flowering herbs are safe to use. To decorate the cake, put the flowers in green stem holders used by florists; fill the holders halfway with water, and push them into the baked cake after it's frosted. Stick the stems into the holders, and the flowers will stay fresh all day long.

14. Make a small bouquet of flowers (rinse and dry them) for a decoration. Tie the bouquet with a ribbon, and lay it on top of the cake. Or arrange flowers on top of the cake, covering the stems with the leaves.

15. Wrap a ribbon around a cake like a package, anchoring the ends of the ribbon with a little frosting. Tie a bow, pierce it with a toothpick, and attach it to the cake where the ends of the ribbon meet. Push the toothpick into the cake so it doesn't show.

16. Make an ice-cream cake. Line any cake pan with plastic wrap. Spoon your favorite ice cream, slightly softened, into the pan. Press the ice cream into the pan so it fills all the corners; smooth the top of the ice cream with a metal spatula. Freeze the ice cream until it's firm, about one hour. Meanwhile bake one layer of a cake in the same-size pan. Remove the cake from the pan, and allow it to cool. To unmold the ice cream, run a spatula around the edges of the pan; turn it upside down on a freezer-proof cake plate. Top the ice cream with the cake layer, frost them quickly, and add decorations. Freeze the cake until you're ready to serve it.

# Holidays

## JANUARY

**1:** New Year's Day

**6:** Epiphany, or Twelfth Day (Many Christians celebrate the visit of the wise men, which is observed twelve days after Christmas.)

**15:** Martin Luther King, Jr.'s Birthday

**Third Monday in January:** Martin Luther King, Jr.'s Birthday observed

**January or February:** Chinese New Year (This holiday always begins at sunset on the day of the second new moon following the winter solstice, between January 21 and February 19.)

## FEBRUARY

**1:** National Freedom Day (This holiday commemorates the signing of the Thirteenth Amendment to abolish slavery.)

**2:** Groundhog Day

**12:** Lincoln's Birthday

**14:** Valentine's Day

**22:** Washington's Birthday

**Third Monday in February:** Presidents' Day

## MARCH

**17:** Saint Patrick's Day

**March or April:** Passover (It is celebrated on the fourteenth of Nisan according to the Jewish lunar calendar.)

**Sunday before Easter:** Palm Sunday

**Friday before Easter:** Good Friday

**March or April:** Easter Sunday

**Monday after Easter:** Easter Monday (This day is a legal holiday in Canada.)

## APRIL

**1:** April Fools' Day

**Third Sunday in April:** Earth Day

**Last Friday in April:** Arbor Day

**Fourth week in April:** Professional Secretaries Week (It is celebrated the entire week, but Secretaries Day is on Wednesday.)

## MAY

**1:** May Day

**First Thursday in May:** The National Day of Prayer

**Tuesday of the first full week of May:** National Teacher Day

**5:** Cinco de Mayo (This national holiday recognizes the victory of Mexican troops over invading French troops at the Battle of Puebla on May 5, 1862.)

**Second Sunday in May:** Mother's Day

**Third Saturday in May:** Armed Forces Day

**First Monday preceding May 25:** Victoria Day (This holiday commemorates the birth of Queen Victoria.)

**Last Monday in May:** Memorial Day observed

**30:** Memorial Day

# Holidays

## JUNE

**14:** Flag Day

**Third Sunday in June:** Father's Day

## JULY

**1:** Canada Day (This national holiday celebrates Canada's birthday.)

**4:** Independence Day

## SEPTEMBER

**First Monday in September:** Labor Day (This federal public holiday is also observed in Canada.)

**First Sunday after Labor Day:** Grandparents Day

**17:** Citizenship Day (This day is set aside to stress the rights and obligations the Constitution gives every American citizen.)

**September or October:** Rosh Hashanah (This is the Jewish New Year and is observed on the first and second days of Tishri.)

**September or October:** Yom Kippur, or Day of Atonement (This Jewish holiday is observed on the tenth of Tishri; a day of atonement for sin, it is observed with fasting and prayer.)

## OCTOBER

**Second Monday in October:** Columbus Day observed

**16:** Boss's Day, or National Boss Day (If October 16 falls on a weekend, it is celebrated on the Friday closest to this date.)

**Last Sunday in October:** Mother-in-Law's Day

**31:** Halloween

## NOVEMBER

**Tuesday after the first Monday in November:** Election Day

**11:** Veterans Day

**Fourth Thursday in November:** Thanksgiving Day

**November or December:** Hanukkah (This eight-day Jewish feast begins on the twenty-fifth day of Kislev.)

## DECEMBER

**1:** First Day of Advent

**25:** Christmas Day

**The first weekday after Christmas:** Boxing Day (It is a legal holiday in Canada when Christmas boxes [gifts] are given to public service employees.)

**31:** New Year's Eve

# Holiday and Special Occasion Planner

**Occasion** _____

**Date:** _____  **Time:** _____  **Place:** _____

### Guests

_____  _____  _____
_____  _____  _____
_____  _____  _____
_____  _____  _____
_____  _____  _____

### Food

_____  _____
_____  _____
_____  _____
_____  _____
_____  _____

### Decorations and Party Favors

_____  _____
_____  _____
_____  _____
_____  _____
_____  _____

### Activities, Crafts and/or Games

_____  _____
_____  _____
_____  _____
_____  _____

# Celebration Planning Calendar

## January

| Date | Holiday or Occasion | Plans or Activity |
|------|---------------------|-------------------|
| 1st | New Year's Day | Chili Bowl Party |
|  |  |  |
| 22nd | Folks' Anniversary | Decorate Cake |
|  |  |  |
|  |  |  |

## February

| Date | Holiday or Occasion | Plans or Activity |
|------|---------------------|-------------------|
|  |  |  |
| 13th | Dad's Birthday | Family Dinner |
| 14th | Valentine's Day | Make Cherry-Pecan Cookies |
|  |  |  |
|  |  |  |

## March

| Date | Holiday or Occasion | Plans or Activity |
|------|---------------------|-------------------|
| 1st | James's Birthday | Circus Party |
| 10th | Joel's Birthday | This is Your Life Party |
| 24th | Grandma's Birthday | Party at Aunt Sandy's |
| 29th | Good Friday | Church 7:00 p.m. |
| 31st | Easter | Make Confetti Eggs Egg Hunt |

## April

| Date | Holiday or Occasion | Plans or Activity |
|------|---------------------|-------------------|
|  |  |  |
| 22nd | Granddaddy's Birthday | Send card and gift |
| 22nd | Earth Day | Make Sculptures and dirt cake |
|  |  |  |
|  |  |  |

## May

| Date | Holiday or Occasion | Plans or Activity |
|------|---------------------|-------------------|
| 1st | May Day | Make flower Piñatas |
| 12th | Mother's Day | Dad makes Breakfast |
|  |  |  |
|  |  |  |
| 31st | Memorial Day | Host a Kite-Flying Party |

## June

| Date | Holiday or Occasion | Plans or Activity |
|------|---------------------|-------------------|
| 1st | Uncle Fred's Birthday | Send a gift |
|  |  |  |
| 14th | Flag Day | Make Stars-and-stripes Wind Sock |
| 21st | Father's Day | Kids make gift coupons |
|  |  |  |

# Celebration Planning Calendar

## January

| Date | Holiday or Occasion | Plans or Activity |
|------|---------------------|-------------------|
| ___ | _____ | _____ |
| ___ | _____ | _____ |
| ___ | _____ | _____ |
| ___ | _____ | _____ |
| ___ | _____ | _____ |
| ___ | _____ | _____ |

## February

| Date | Holiday or Occasion | Plans or Activity |
|------|---------------------|-------------------|
| ___ | _____ | _____ |
| ___ | _____ | _____ |
| ___ | _____ | _____ |
| ___ | _____ | _____ |
| ___ | _____ | _____ |
| ___ | _____ | _____ |

## March

| Date | Holiday or Occasion | Plans or Activity |
|------|---------------------|-------------------|
| ___ | _____ | _____ |
| ___ | _____ | _____ |
| ___ | _____ | _____ |
| ___ | _____ | _____ |
| ___ | _____ | _____ |
| ___ | _____ | _____ |

## April

| Date | Holiday or Occasion | Plans or Activity |
|------|---------------------|-------------------|
| ___ | _____ | _____ |
| ___ | _____ | _____ |
| ___ | _____ | _____ |
| ___ | _____ | _____ |
| ___ | _____ | _____ |
| ___ | _____ | _____ |

## May

| Date | Holiday or Occasion | Plans or Activity |
|------|---------------------|-------------------|
| ___ | _____ | _____ |
| ___ | _____ | _____ |
| ___ | _____ | _____ |
| ___ | _____ | _____ |
| ___ | _____ | _____ |
| ___ | _____ | _____ |

## June

| Date | Holiday or Occasion | Plans or Activity |
|------|---------------------|-------------------|
| ___ | _____ | _____ |
| ___ | _____ | _____ |
| ___ | _____ | _____ |
| ___ | _____ | _____ |
| ___ | _____ | _____ |
| ___ | _____ | _____ |

| July | | | | August | | |
|------|------|------|------|------|------|------|
| Date | Holiday or Occasion | Plans or Activity | Date | Holiday or Occasion | Plans or Activity | |
| _____ | _____ | _____ | _____ | _____ | _____ | |
| _____ | _____ | _____ | _____ | _____ | _____ | |
| _____ | _____ | _____ | _____ | _____ | _____ | |
| _____ | _____ | _____ | _____ | _____ | _____ | |
| _____ | _____ | _____ | _____ | _____ | _____ | |
| _____ | _____ | _____ | _____ | _____ | _____ | |

| September | | | | October | | |
|------|------|------|------|------|------|------|
| Date | Holiday or Occasion | Plans or Activity | Date | Holiday or Occasion | Plans or Activity | |
| _____ | _____ | _____ | _____ | _____ | _____ | |
| _____ | _____ | _____ | _____ | _____ | _____ | |
| _____ | _____ | _____ | _____ | _____ | _____ | |
| _____ | _____ | _____ | _____ | _____ | _____ | |
| _____ | _____ | _____ | _____ | _____ | _____ | |
| _____ | _____ | _____ | _____ | _____ | _____ | |

| November | | | | December | | |
|------|------|------|------|------|------|------|
| Date | Holiday or Occasion | Plans or Activity | Date | Holiday or Occasion | Plans or Activity | |
| _____ | _____ | _____ | _____ | _____ | _____ | |
| _____ | _____ | _____ | _____ | _____ | _____ | |
| _____ | _____ | _____ | _____ | _____ | _____ | |
| _____ | _____ | _____ | _____ | _____ | _____ | |
| _____ | _____ | _____ | _____ | _____ | _____ | |
| _____ | _____ | _____ | _____ | _____ | _____ | |

**Chapter 2**

# Winter Holidays

Fun celebrations abound for every national holiday. We've included lots of creative activities to make these times special, plus we've added fun ideas from our own families' encyclopedia of commemorations. We hope these suggestions will help you plan yours and stimulate you to create some of your own.

**"Oh the weather outside is frightful
But the fire is so delightful,
And since we've no place to go,
Let it Snow! Let it Snow! Let it Snow!"**

*Sammy Cahn*

## First Day of Winter: December

Winter solstice, about December 21, marks the first day of winter and is the shortest day of the year. Daylight ranges from twelve hours at the equator to zero at the Arctic Circle.

1. Make yarn snowflakes. Dip a 36-inch length of yarn into white glue. Arrange the yarn in a snowflake shape on a piece of waxed paper. When the yarn is dry, peel the snowflake away from the waxed paper. Paint a light coat of glue on each side of the snowflake, and sprinkle it with glitter. Make a hanger from a loop of thread or dental floss, and hang the snowflake in a window.

2. Feed the birds during the winter months. Make bird feeders from an orange. Cut the orange in two, and remove the pulp from both halves. Make three small holes evenly spaced around the top rim of each orange cup. Thread and knot a 10-inch length of string into each one of the holes of an orange cup. Tie the three loose ends together in a knot to form a hanger. Do the same with the other orange cup. Fill the oranges with birdseed, and hang them.

3. Fix pancakes for breakfast today. When it's cold outside, the kids will have fun making this easy syrup.

**Homemade Maple Syrup**

½ cup water

1 cup sugar

1 teaspoon vanilla

1 teaspoon maple flavoring

Place water and sugar in a small saucepan, cooking them over medium heat until the sugar is dissolved. Do not stir (this causes crystals); gently shake the pan. When sugar is dissolved, remove pan from heat, and stir in flavorings.

4. Let your child help you make the following hot beverage mixes to keep on hand for your family to enjoy all winter.

### Hot Buttered Apple Cider Mix

1 pound brown sugar

½ cup butter

1 teaspoon cinnamon

½ teaspoon ground cloves

¼ teaspoon ground nutmeg

Cream sugar, butter and spices in a medium-size bowl until smooth. Put mix in a covered container; store in the refrigerator for up to 6 weeks. To serve, place 1 heaping tablespoon of mixture in a mug, and fill with simmering apple cider.

### Hot Chocolate Mix

1 cup cocoa powder

2½ cups powdered sugar

2 cups dry, nondairy coffee creamer

2 cups nonfat dry milk powder

Mix all the ingredients. Store mix in a self-locking plastic bag. To serve, place 3 tablespoons chocolate mix in a mug, and then fill it with ¾ cup boiling water.

# New Year's Eve: December 31

The evening before the first day of the new year is a festive night of celebration. When the clock strikes midnight, "Auld Lang Syne" is traditionally sung while fireworks explode, horns blow, and loved ones embrace.

1. Ask each family member to give his or her opinion about the year's best: blessing, book, news, family event or outing, song, movie or TV program. Be sure to record and save the answers. It's fun to get those answers out years later and see how times have changed.

2. Invite other families to your home for a watch party. Play games to pass the time until midnight. One family we know invites other families over to play charades on New Year's Eve. At midnight they make pancakes and fix other breakfast fare. The children love to stay up late on this special evening.

3. For the countdown to midnight, make a large clock from poster board. Use a metal brad to secure movable clock hands. Let younger children move the hands corresponding to the correct time. Kids will also enjoy decorating the top of a cake to look like the face of a clock. (Frosting tubes with writing tips are available in the baking aisle of grocery stores.)

4. Make Roman confetti candles. Cover empty cardboard paper towel rolls with a 17-inch length of aluminum foil. Allow 3 inches to hang over each end of the roll. Close one end of the tube with the foil. Fill tube with confetti. Twist foil at the open end to look like a candle wick. To shoot off candles, let children hold the roll at the closed end and swing it around. Watch the confetti sparks fly.

5. Help your kids fix delicious warm-milk beverages for a late-night treat.

**Hot Almond Milk**

1 cup milk

2 tablespoons sugar

1½ teaspoons almond flavoring

Heat milk in a small saucepan just until it begins to simmer. Remove pan from heat, and stir in sugar and almond flavoring until it dissolves. Pour milk into a mug, and serve it hot.

6. Serve interesting coffee beverages to the adults to help them stay awake!

**Cocoa Mocha Punch**

1 16-ounce can chocolate syrup

1 2-ounce jar instant coffee

1 cup sugar

1 quart boiling water

Combine the chocolate syrup, coffee, sugar and boiling water in a 1-gallon (heat resistant) container, stirring until sugar is dissolved. Finish filling container with cool water. This makes 1 gallon of punch base. To make the drink, mix equal amounts of punch base and milk, and serve it over ice.

# New Year's Day: January 1

Observing the new year dates back to pre-Christian times when rites were performed to ensure the return of spring.[1] January 1 became generally recognized as New Year's Day in the 1500s when the Gregorian calendar was first introduced. The British Calendar Act of 1751 pro-claimed this day officially as the beginning of the year in most English-speaking countries. Traditionally, New Year's Day is a time for personal evaluation and for making resolutions for the coming year.

1. Make a family cassette or video tape recording on January 1. In one family, both the parents and kids set goals for how they want to grow intellectually, physically, spiritually and financially over the coming year. Then the following January 1, they play the cassette tape back, evaluate their progress and make a new tape for the next year. Encourage your family to think about and write their goals before you record them.

2. Deliver New Year's gifts as a family. If Christmas passed before you had time to see certain friends, it's not too late to give a season's greeting. Soak the label off empty, clean, 1-quart mayonnaise jars. Use paint pens to draw confetti and balloons on the jars, and write "Happy New Year's." Fill the jars with candies your family has made.

3. Begin a new hobby or collection, or learn a new craft. Fun hobbies for kids include collecting coins or stamps, learning to cross stitch, or building a doll house or models. Be sure to have the necessary kits or supplies so you can start on the first day of the year.

4. Start a scrapbook for the new year. Your children can decorate an inexpensive notebook or album. Use gift wrapping paper, self-stick or regular fabric and braided or lace trim or ribbons. Lay the notebook on the paper or fabric, and fold

it over the edges of the notebook, leaving a 1-inch allowance. Cut the paper or fabric, and fold it over the edges, attaching it to the inside of the covers with a glue gun or tacky craft glue. Cut matching pieces of paper or fabric to fit the inside front and back covers, and glue them in place, covering the raw edges. Glue trim and ribbon on the outside in pretty designs.

Your children can use this book throughout the year to collect and save mementos from school and special events, letters from friends and relatives and other treasures. One mom said that she weekly added items to her three young children's scrapbooks. As they grew older, they began a Sunday afternoon ritual of gluing papers and items in their own scrapbooks. They also wrote about the week's events. They now have stacks of scrapbooks filled with great memories.

5. Host a chili bowl party. Invite other families to watch the bowl games and eat chili on New Year's Day. Decorate with balloons and crepe paper in your favorite teams' colors. Let children make pennants from construction paper. Older kids can compose cheers and team yells. Mom and Dad may enjoy sharing some of the team cheers from high school and college days. But be prepared for the kids to think they're corny!

Cheerleading has become more sophisticated since the days of:

"Pork chop, pork chop,
  Greasy, greasy,
We'll beat your team
  Easy, easy!"

6. Play Crazy Cookie Chaos at halftime. To prepare for the game, buy a package of Chinese fortune cookies. Carefully remove paper fortunes from the cookies with tweezers. Replace fortunes with instructions for silly stunts. For example: Sing "Old MacDonald Had a Farm" to the tune of "The Star Spangled Banner." Act as if you're an aerobic flamingo, and do ten jumping jacks while standing on one leg. Pretend you're playing the flute or tuba in a marching band; make the sound of your instrument as you march around the room. Eat ten soda crackers; then try to whistle "Yankee Doodle."

Game instructions: Have each participant number off until everyone has been counted. Start with number one, playing in order. The first player chooses a crazy cookie. He or she must break open the cookie and act out the instructions.

The second player has the option of repeating the first player's stunt or choosing a new cookie and performing that stunt. If player number two chooses to perform the first player's stunt, player number one must choose a new cookie and perform another stunt. Each player is limited to three stunts. Repeat this process until all players have performed at least one stunt.

7. Begin the Southern tradition of eating black-eyed peas on New Year's Day. Our families enjoy this recipe:

**Texas Caviar**
3 16-ounce cans black-eyed peas, drained
1 diced bell pepper
1 small onion, chopped
2 ounces diced pimentos, drained
1 clove minced garlic
1 cup Italian salad dressing
2 tablespoons salsa

Combine all the ingredients. Allow black-eyed peas to marinate in a glass jar or plastic container, tightly covered in the refrigerator for 2 to 3 days. Serve as a dip with corn chips or crackers. Makes 2 quarts.

# Martin Luther King Day: The Third Monday in January

In 1986, this day in January was designated as a public holiday in memory of Martin Luther King, Jr. King was a black civil rights leader, minister and recipient of the Nobel Peace Prize in 1964. He stressed brotherhood and non-violence.

At the Lincoln Memorial, in Washington, D.C., on August 28, 1963, King delivered his famous speech entitled "I Have a Dream." In that speech he said: "I have a dream that one day . . . , the sons of former slaves and the sons of former slave owners will be able to sit down together at the table of brotherhood. . . . I have a dream that my four little children will one day live in a nation where they will not be judged by the color of their skin but by the content of their character."[2]

1. Talk to your children about the meaning of the word *prejudice*. Then brainstorm about some ways we can develop friendships and learn from people of different races or political persuasions. Ask these questions: What are some ways you can bridge the gap between children of other races in our own neighborhood? How can you make friends with children who are different from you or speak another language?

2. Talk about dreams and goals with your family at dinner on this holiday, reading the following quotes aloud and using them for discussion starters:

"Nothing much happens without a dream. For something really great to happen, it takes a really great dream." Robert Greenleaf[3]

"If you can dream it, you can do it." Walt Disney[4]

3. Check out books from the library, and learn about the cultures of children with different nationalities in your own community.

4. Watch your local newspaper for parades or historical exhibitions taking place in your city on this day, and attend them as a family.

# Groundhog Day: February 2

Groundhog Day stems from an American legend started by Pennsylvania Germans. The tradition says that if the groundhog sees its shadow when it emerges from its burrow on February 2, it will be frightened, crawl back into its hole, and winter weather will continue for six more weeks. If the day is cloudy and the groundhog doesn't see its shadow, winter is supposed to end soon.

1. Make groundhog puppets. Use a brown crayon or marker to color the outside of a white, 10-ounce Styrofoam cup. Poke a hole with a pencil the size of a plastic drinking straw in the center bottom of the cup. Color a 2-inch Styrofoam ball

to look like the head of a groundhog, gluing small felt pieces on the ball for facial features and ears. Push one end of a straw into the neck part of the head, and the other end of the straw through the hole in the cup. Holding the cup right-side up, pull the straw down; the groundhog's head will disappear inside the cup. Push the straw up and down to pretend the groundhog is coming out of its hole.

2. Create a make-believe story with your child about Groundhog Day. Your characters might be Gregory Groundhog, Sissy Squirrel and Rebecca Rabbit. Take turns making up the events of the story.

3. Let your child make his or her own burrow to play in. You can cover a card table with a blanket or get a large appliance box from a furniture or appliance store to make the burrow.

4. Eat sunshine sandwiches for lunch today. Cut sandwich bread into circles. Spread with egg salad. Use two stuffed green olive halves for eyes and pimento pieces to shape a smiling mouth.

# Valentine's Day: February 14

This holiday began as a celebration honoring two Christian saints, both named Valentine. They were martyred by the Roman Emperor Claudius. Since the Middle Ages, the day has been dedicated to lovers, probably because it was believed to be the day birds chose their mates.[5]

1. Wake your children in a special way today.

Say "I love you" in a way that is meaningful to each child. One child may enjoy a back scratch upon waking, and another might enjoy smelling the aroma of his or her favorite breakfast coming from the kitchen.

2. Make up silly "Roses are red" verses about each other. Be prepared for some laughter!

3. Have a Valentine's Day treasure hunt. Give your children the first clue, which leads to another clue somewhere in your home. Make up about five or six clues, with the last one leading them to a gift.

4. Start a yearly tradition of making your child a Valentine's Day surprise box. Use Valentine gift paper to separately wrap the outside of a square box and a matching lid. Glue heart-shaped doilies or Valentine greeting cards on the sides and lid of the box. Attach small heart stickers and Valentine decorations on top of the doilies. Fill the decorated box with candies, gum, a small stuffed animal or other Valentine treats. Put the lid on the box, and tie it with a red ribbon, making a bow on top.

5. Create a Valentine's post office from a large furniture or appliance box. Cut a window in the front. Then paint it red and white, and decorate it with hearts. Let younger neighborhood children exchange Valentine's cards, taking turns as the post office worker.

6. Make a Valentine's Day lace wreath with your children. Cut a 12-inch circle from cardboard. Then cut a 6-inch circle from the center

of the 12-inch circle. Purchase 3 yards of gathered lace 2½-inches wide. Wind the lace around and through the wreath form, overlapping layers until the cardboard is completely covered. (It should look like a layered, ruffled skirt.) Glue both ends of the lace to the back of the wreath. Decorate the wreath by gluing red-ribbon bows, small flowers, hearts or other trim to it. Hang the wreath on your door or mantle, or give it as a gift.

7. Use old-fashioned paper doilies for place mats to dress up your table.

8. Describe at dinner tonight how you and your spouse met. Let the children ask questions about your courtship. Look at your wedding pictures as a family.

9. Fix this fun red sauce as a dip for sliced, fresh fruits and vegetables:

**Rosy Red Sauce**

¾ cup frozen sweetened raspberries, thawed and drained
¼ cup lemon juice
¾ cup sour cream

Place raspberries and lemon juice into a food processor or blender, and process until smooth. Put the sour cream in a medium-size serving bowl. Gently fold raspberry mixture into the sour cream. Cover the bowl and refrigerate until serving time. Serve with slices of apples, oranges, pears, bananas, carrots or celery. Makes 1¾ cups.

10. Let your kids make these easy cookies.

**Cherry-Pecan Cookies**

1 34-ounce package refrigerated cookie dough
½ cup chopped maraschino cherries
½ cup chopped pecans

Preheat oven to 350⁰. Unwrap cookie dough, and place it in a medium bowl. Using your hands, mix the cherries and pecans into the dough. Drop dough by teaspoonfuls onto lightly greased cookie sheets. Bake for 6 to 8 minutes or until golden brown. Makes about 4 dozen.

**Note**: You may also add chocolate chips, raisins or crushed peppermint candy to make refrigerated cookie dough taste like homemade.

# Presidents' Day: The Third Monday in February

This day was originally set aside to honor Presidents Washington and Lincoln. George Washington (1732-99), our country's first president, is called the father of his country. Abraham Lincoln (1809-65) was the sixteenth president. He gave the nation spiritual, moral and political leadership during the difficult years of the Civil War. In the Emancipation Proclamation, issued on January 1, 1863, he freed all slaves in the United States.

Although the third Monday in February has been set to observe the birthdays of those two great presidents, it has also become a day to honor all the presidents of the United States.

1. Let your child pretend to be president for the day, calling him or her "Mr. or Madam President." Make a top secret briefcase. Paint an old lunch box black or brown. Make sturdy cardboard dividers and pockets for the inside to hold pens,

pencils and a confidential notebook. Allow your child to make executive household decisions, such as the dinner menu and what game to play as a family tonight.

2. Start a dinner table discussion, asking these questions: What character qualities are needed to be a good president? Would you like to be president of the United States? Why or why not?

3. Collect interesting trivia about past presidents from history books and encyclopedias, and create a guessing game for your family. For example, one of the questions could be: Who was the first U.S. president to have a telephone on his desk? (The answer is Herbert Hoover. "Prior to 1929, the president used a telephone booth outside his office!"[6])

4. Watch the Public Broadcasting System's series "The Civil War" to learn more about the history of America during Lincoln's presidency. Check with your local library or video rental store to obtain the tapes, or call 1-800-424-7963 to order the series. The movie *Shenandoah* is also a good family movie to watch about the Civil War.

5. Fix Gettysburgers for dinner tonight (hamburgers with **Secret Service Sauce**). Serve with **Copper Penny Salad**.

### Secret Service Sauce
½ cup mayonnaise
2 tablespoons ketchup
2 tablespoons pickle relish

Mix all ingredients, put sauce in a covered container, and refrigerate until ready to serve hamburgers. Makes about ¾ cup sauce.

### Copper Penny Salad
2 cups sliced carrots
½ cup raisins
¼ cup mayonnaise

Slice carrots into thin rounds. Mix all ingredients. Serve on salad greens if desired. Makes 4½ cup servings.

**Note**: Show young children President Lincoln's image on pennies and the presidents on other coins and bills.

# Saint Patrick's Day: March 17

This day commemorates Saint Patrick, the patron saint of Ireland. He introduced Christianity to Ireland about A.D. 432, using a shamrock to represent the Holy Trinity. In the United States, we celebrate this holiday with parades and by wearing green, the color of the shamrock. An old tradition says that if you see people not wearing something green on this day, you may pinch them.

1. Serve green eggs and ham for breakfast. Make scrambled eggs as usual, except use a few drops of food coloring to tint them green. Serve with cooked breakfast ham.

2. Have a penny hunt. Have the children wrap pennies in gold foil. Then hide them in a sandbox or a small grassy area of your yard. Children can pretend to be leprechauns and search for the golden nugget pennies. Allow children five minutes to find all the pennies they can, which

they can keep for prizes.

3. Have a green party. Send green invitations. Ask your guests to wear green clothes. Decorate with green balloons and crepe paper.

a. Fill a quart jar with green jelly beans. As the guests arrive, ask them to guess how many beans are in the jar. Write down their guesses. Whoever guesses closest to the actual number of jelly beans gets to take them home.

b. Play the Secret Leprechaun game at your party. This is fun for kids ages three to ninety-three.

Let the host or hostess designate one person to be the leprechaun, and escort this person to a soundproof location. At this time the host or hostess explains the secret procedure to the leprechaun. When the host or hostess asks about a green object right before asking about the correct object, that will be the leprechaun's clue that the next item is the one the group has chosen.

While the leprechaun is still out of the room, the host or hostess asks the remaining guests to choose one visible item in the room for the leprechaun to try to guess. After the item is decided upon, the leprechaun is brought back into the room. The host or hostess then names a series of objects, and the leprechaun guesses whether or not an object is the item the guests have named.

The process is repeated until someone in the group guesses the system by whispering the secret to the host or hostess (so the rest of the group can figure out the trick on their own). Then let that person be the leprechaun until more people catch on. Keep playing the game until several others have guessed the trick.

1. John W. Wright, ed., *The Universal Almanac 1990* (Kansas City: Andrews & McMeel, 1989), 15.
2. John Bartlett, *Familiar Quotations* (Boston: Little, Brown & Co., 1980), 909.
3. Ann McGee-Cooper, *You Don't Have to Go Home from Work Exhausted!* (Dallas: Bowen & Rogers Publishing Co., 1990), 26.
4. Ibid., 28.
5. Wright, *The Universal Almanac 1990*, 16.
6. Karin De Venuta, comp., "Facts & Figures," *The Wall Street Journal* (November 9, 1990): R5.

# Chapter 3

# Spring Holidays

## First Day of Spring: March

The first day of spring, about March 21, is set on the vernal equinox. The sun rises due east and sets due west except near the poles. The lengths of day and night are virtually the same everywhere.[1]

1. Let your children begin a garden by making seed flats. Cut 9 inches off the top of a gallon plastic milk carton. Fill the carton 2 inches deep with a mixture of half potting soil and half peat moss. Plant seeds according to seed packet instructions. Keep soil moist. When plants are three to four inches high and the last frost is over, transplant seedlings into an outside garden plot. Good seeds to start are beans, tomatoes, cucumbers, peppers and herbs.

**"Surprises are happening under the snow. Down deep in the ground things are starting to grow . . . . Yes, Spring's on the way with its wonderful show. Surprises are happening under the snow!"**
*Jean Conder Soule*

2. Go sledding without snow. Obtain a large box from a furniture or appliance store. Flatten the box, and find a grassy hill to slide down.

3. Celebrate the end of winter by visiting a park and playing this string-puzzle game. Using a long ball of string, tie the loose end to a starting point. Walk the path you want your children to take, unraveling the string as you go. Put a treat or reward at the end of the string. Beginning at the starting point, let your children follow the course of the string and wind it back into a ball as they go.

4. Fix **Sunny Spring Salad** for dinner. Place a scoop of cottage cheese on a salad plate, and surround it with pineapple chunks or peach slices to make it look like a sun. Or make a flower by

adding a celery stalk or carrot stick for the stem. Place a maraschino cherry in the middle of the cottage cheese for the center of the flower.

# Spring Cleaning Day

Make spring cleaning a family celebration. You may want to make this a surprise holiday so your children won't have a chance to run away from home!

Do some beforehand planning. Collect boxes for packing seasonal clothes that need to be stored and items that are still in good condition and can be passed on to others. Make sure you have necessary cleaning supplies on hand.

1. Post a list of specific cleaning assignments for each family member. After each task is completed, give younger children a sticker. Older children can mark off finished chores on a list. When the list is completed, go out for a treat.

2. Play basketball clean-up. Station laundry baskets, boxes, clothes hampers and trash cans in strategic locations around the house. Label each receptacle according to what you want to end up in it, and let the kids gently toss in clothes that they have outgrown, unbreakable items and trash into their respective containers. Designate one person to be in charge of sorting through and folding the clothing items that will be stored or given away. Unusable clothing can be cut up for rags, and the buttons can be cut off for crafts.

3. Set up a cash-and-carry incentive for older kids to do larger jobs. For instance, give a small cash reward for helping to move furniture back and forth or for carrying all the boxes to the attic or carrying mounds of garbage bags to the proper trash pick-up location.

4. Take a picture of your child in front of a project he or she has done especially well. Mount the picture on a half sheet of construction paper. Write a caption under the picture such as: "Thanks for the hard work!" or "A Job Well Done!" Tape the picture to the door of your refrigerator for a week or two.

5. Have your kids fix **Power Punch** and **Texas Trash** to snack on and keep them going on spring cleaning day.

### Power Punch

Mix 1 can frozen orange juice concentrate and club soda in the amount suggested for water on the juice can.

### Texas Trash

½ cup butter
2 tablespoons Worcestershire sauce
2 teaspoons seasoned salt
1 cup pretzel sticks
1 cup O-shaped oat cereal
1 cup square cheese crackers
1 cup square-shaped rice cereal
1 cup square-shaped wheat cereal
1 cup bite-size shredded wheat cereal
1 cup bite-size wheat crackers
1 cup bite-size butter crackers
1 cup assorted nuts

Preheat oven to 325°. Combine butter, Worcestershire sauce and your favorite seasoning salt in a small saucepan. Heat mixture until butter is melted, stirring constantly. Combine remaining ingredients in a large bowl. Pour melted butter over dry mixture, stirring to coat evenly. Spread snack mix in rimmed cookie sheets. Bake for 25 to 30 minutes or until lightly brown, stirring every 10 minutes. Cool snack mix, and store it in an airtight container. Makes 9 cups.

# April Fools' Day: April 1

For centuries, this day has been recognized as a day to play practical jokes on each other. The origin of this day is obscure, but it's a great day to incorporate humor into your regular schedule.

1. Pack a silly sack lunch for your child today. Fix a trick sandwich by putting a piece of bread between two pieces of lunch meat. Send pink hard-boiled eggs (soak hard-boiled eggs in pickled beet juice), an apple with a candy gummy worm sticking out of the side and Christmas cookies for dessert.

2. Help younger children make an April Fools' jack-in-the-box. Get an empty, clean peanut can with a plastic, snap-top lid. Then cut a strip of paper 2 inches wide and three times as long as the can is tall; fold strip back and forth in 1 inch intervals to make a paper spring. Put a few peanuts and the spring inside the can, and cover it with the lid. Your child will have fun offering the can to family members or friends. Little kids love to think they're fooling older people!

3. Let your children trick their friends with a box of baby rattlers. Put several baby rattle toys in a medium-size box with a lid. Attach a sign to the outside of the box that says: DANGER! BABY RATTLERS INSIDE.

4. Invite other families over for a Lirpa Sloof Backward Party. Write the invitations backward. Ask the guests to wear their clothes backward. Make place cards with the guests' names spelled backward. On the back of each place card, write a joke or riddle for the person to take a turn reading during dinner. Eat dessert first and salad last. For small children, have a backward parade, marching backward. Older children can play relay games walking and running backward. Greet your guests by saying "Good-bye."

# Passover: March or April

Passover, the Jewish feast of freedom, is celebrated on the fourteenth of the Jewish month of Nisan (March or April). It's a celebration and memorial of God's deliverance of the Jews from slavery in Egypt. The name *Passover* also recalls God's sparing (passing over) the Jewish first-born sons during the plagues on Egypt brought by God through Moses. The holiday is marked by eating only unleavened foods and participating in a Seder meal.[2] Each food item on the Seder plate is symbolic of the time the Israelites left Egypt and went into the desert on their way to the promised land.

1. Read chapters seven through twelve of Exodus aloud to your family from a modern translation of the Bible. You may want to read one chapter each night during the Passover week.

2. Rent the movie *The Ten Commandments* from a local video store. Watch it as a family, and talk about what you learned about Jewish heritage and history. You may also want to read a book

about the life of Moses and how he was used by God to deliver the Jews from bondage in Egypt.

3. For more information about Passover, read *Jewish Holidays and Festivals*, by Isidor Margolis and Rabbi Sidney L. Marowitz.

4. Fix **Haroseth**, a sweet mixture of chopped apples and nuts. This dish is a part of the Seder meal that represents the bricks and mortar the Jews used to build the pharaoh's cities while they were slaves.

### Haroseth

2 cups chopped apples
½ cup chopped nuts
2 teaspoons cinnamon
2 tablespoons honey or sugar

Mix all ingredients in a medium-size bowl. Cover the bowl, and refrigerate it. Serve **Haroseth** as a salad, or spread it on matzo crackers for a snack.

# Easter: March or April

Christians consider this the most joyous day of the year. Easter commemorates the resurrection of Jesus Christ from death to life. It falls on the first Sunday after the first full moon following the vernal equinox (the first day of spring), sometime between March 22 and April 25. Many churches decorate with white lilies to symbolize purity and light.

The tradition of wearing new clothes for Easter evolved from celebrating the earth dressed in a fresh cloak of greenery and flowers. The custom of the Easter rabbit and eggs came from ancient Egypt and Persia. The eggs are a symbol of new life.

1. Read the Easter story (John 18-20) aloud to older children from a modern translation of the Bible. Read to younger children the Easter story from a children's Bible storybook. Children of all ages will enjoy *The Lion, the Witch and the Wardrobe,* by C. S. Lewis, (read a chapter a night aloud) the week before Easter. This story is about how Aslan, a noble lion who symbolizes Jesus Christ, frees Narnia from the spell of the White Witch.

2. Conduct your own Easter sunrise service at a park or scenic location where you can watch the sun rise. If that's not convenient because of Easter church service times, you can do it on Palm Sunday (the Sunday before Easter) to prepare for the week. One of the Peels' special memories is the time they had an early morning breakfast and family service at a state park. They collected stones, built a small altar by stacking the stones under a tree, and had a time of Bible reading and family prayer. The next time they visited the park, they looked for their altar, and it was still there.

3. Early Easter morning, deliver treats, such as chocolate eggs, breakfast cinnamon rolls or cookies, to your neighbors' front doors. Keep them guessing about the identity of the neighborhood Easter bunny.

4. Check your local newspaper for Easter egg hunts in your community. One of Kathy's favorite childhood memories is of dressing up and

attending church as a family, going out for a special Easter lunch, and participating in a local Easter egg hunt. Each year she became more determined to win the hunt by finding the most eggs and putting them in her basket. After four years of defeat, she decided to put down her basket and collect all the eggs she could by holding up the skirt of her dress, which could carry more. She won the contest but got in a little trouble because the dye from the eggs ruined her dress.

5. Make pretend quail eggs with your kids. Hard-boil small chicken eggs. When cool, they should be propped sideways in the egg carton so that as much shell as possible is showing. Dip an old toothbrush into light blue tempera paint. Rubbing the bristles of the brush with your thumbnail, spatter paint on each egg. When the paint is dry, turn the eggs over and spatter the other sides.

Let the kids create a pretty centerpiece, using the quail eggs in a basket lined with green sheet moss (available at your craft store). (The eggs will last about 3 weeks, but don't eat them.)

6. Make confetti eggs. Using a metal skewer or the end of a potato peeler, make a nickel-size hole in one end of a raw egg. Drain the egg white and yolk, and rinse the empty shell with cool water, allowing it to dry in the carton hole-side down. Dye the eggs; then let them dry. Use a funnel to fill the shell with confetti. Glue a round piece of tissue paper over the hole to seal it, and let your kids have confetti egg wars in the backyard. (Play "rake up the mess" when the war is over!)

7. Make molded Easter baskets. Let your kids make several small baskets to fill with treats for their friends.

### Molded-Sugar Easter Baskets
5 cups granulated sugar
1 egg white

Combine sugar and egg white, kneading with hand for about 1 minute. This sugar mixture can be colored by adding a few drops of food coloring while kneading. Pack a thick layer of the sugar mixture around the outside of a bowl that has been turned upside down. Allow sugar to dry until it's hard, about 5 hours. Carefully remove dried sugar form from bowl. Fill molded Easter basket with candy eggs or small toys. For a centerpiece, fill basket with decorated eggs.

8. Fix gelatin Easter eggs. Use a pointed object, such as the tip of a carrot peeler, to tap a small hole in the top of three or four fresh, raw eggs. Using your fingers, pull away enough shell to make a hole in each one about the size of a dime. Drain the egg white and yolk. Rinse the empty shells carefully with water. Place eggs hole-side down in the egg carton, and allow them to dry overnight. Prepare 1 3-ounce package of flavored gelatin, using only ½ cup hot water and ½ cup cold. Turn eggs hole-side up in the carton, and use a small funnel to fill eggs with liquid gelatin. Refrigerate eggs until firm. Unmold eggs by tapping the shells, holding them under lukewarm water and peeling them as you would a hard-boiled egg. Refrigerate gelatin eggs in an airtight container until you're ready to use them. Serve them on lettuce leaves.

9. Have an old-fashioned egg toss outside. Begin with the members of each two-person team standing five feet apart. The starting player gently tosses the egg to the player across from him or her. Each time the egg is tossed, the players move back one step until the egg breaks when tossed. (Be sure to wear washable clothes!)

# Earth Day: Third Sunday in April

Environmentalists organized the first Earth Day on April 22, 1970. This is an educational event in schools, offices and parks across America to draw attention to the need for reclaiming and preserving the purity of the air, water and living environment.

1. Give your family a litter test. Ask them to guess how long the following items continue to litter the environment when they are thrown out in an irresponsible way:
Paper (2-4 weeks)
Disposable diaper (12-30 years)
Hard plastic container (20-30 years)
Rubber sole of a shoe (30-50 years)
Aluminum can (200-400 years)
Plastic 6-pack drink holder (450 years)[3]

2. Perform an experiment as a family to learn what things are biodegradable. You will need an apple core, potato peelings, an old plastic toy and a Styrofoam cup. Dig four small holes in a flower bed in your yard. Put each item in a separate hole. Fill the holes with dirt, covering each item completely. Place a marker on the holes so you'll be able to find them again. In two months, remove the dirt and check on the items. The apple core and potato peelings are biodegradable and will have become part of the earth again. The toy and the cup will still be intact because they're not biodegradable.

3. Save paper by having the names of your family members removed from junk mailing lists. This cuts down on the accumulation of trash. Americans receive almost 2 million tons of junk mail each year! Let older children write to companies that send unwanted mail and request that your names be removed from their lists. You can also write to the following address and ask that your name not be sold to mailing list companies: Mail Preference Service, Direct Marketing Association, 2 East 43rd Street, New York, NY 10017.

4. Create recycled junk sculptures. Collect aluminum pie pans, toilet paper and paper towel tubes, straws, facial tissue boxes, empty spice containers, margarine tubs and soda pop cans. Supply white tacky craft glue, string, pipe cleaners and masking tape. Help the kids make a huge sculpture. Paint it with gold or silver spray paint. It would also be fun to have a neighborhood kids' junk-sculpture contest.

5. Make this dip for a snack today in memory of the volcano that shook the earth on May 18, 1980.

**Mount Saint Helens Dip**
1 package of frozen chopped spinach
1 box Knorr Swiss vegetable soup mix
1 cup mayonnaise
1 cup sour cream
1 dark round loaf of bread

Defrost spinach, making sure it's well drained. Mix spinach with the soup mix, mayonnaise and sour cream in a medium-size bowl. Cover bowl and refrigerate dip for 2 hours. Cut a 1-inch slice off the top of the loaf. Hollow out the bread, leaving a thick bread shell. Fill it with dip, and serve it with crackers. Makes 3 cups.

6. Fix an **Earth Day Dirt Cake** for dessert. Kids love making this one!

### Earth Day Dirt Cake

2 3½ ounce packages of instant chocolate pudding

2 cups cold milk

2 cups sour cream

1 cup crushed chocolate wafer cookies

1 cup miniature chocolate chips

Place one whole wafer cookie in the bottom of a new, 5-inch plastic planter to cover the drain hole. Beat pudding mix, milk and sour cream in a medium-size bowl until well blended. Stir in the chocolate chips. Pour pudding into planter. Sprinkle crushed chocolate wafers over pudding for a dirt effect. Insert a 12-inch plastic or silk flower into the center of the pot. Makes 6, ½ cup servings.

# Arbor Day: Last Friday In April

This day promotes the planting of trees. Arbor Day was first observed in the state of Nebraska in 1872. By that time, settlers had cut down most of the trees on the plains. Much of the land had been cleared for farming, and the trees had been used to build homes and for firewood. Arbor Day is a reminder that we need to replenish what we use from the earth.

1. Plant a small tree today. Check with a local nursery to find out what types of trees will grow well in your area. The average American uses seven trees a year in paper, wood and other products made from trees. Altogether, we're using more than 1.5 billion trees a year![4]

2. Buy a tree identification book. Go on a nature hike, and see how many trees you recognize. Collect leaves from each tree, and glue them onto a 9-by-11-inch piece of colored construction paper. Label the leaves. Bind the pages to make a scrapbook by punching holes on one side of the papers; then tie them together with yarn.

3. Hunt for deserted bird nests. Spray nests with disinfectant, and store them in self-locking plastic bags. Buy a bird book and identify each nest. Then make the eggs of the particular bird from modeling clay.

4. Plant a bird nest (that's been deserted) in a flower pot, and cover it with about 1 inch of potting soil. Keep it moist, and watch to see what sprouts.

5. Create twig baskets. Cut about two dozen twigs ¼-inch wide and slightly taller than an empty, 12-ounce orange juice can. Use a low-temperature glue gun to secure twigs around the outside of the can. Make sure twigs are glued as close together as possible. When twigs are set in place, tuck small bits of Spanish moss into spaces between the twigs to fill holes where the can is

showing. Use a wooden pick to push the moss between the twigs. Wrap a piece of raffia around the twigs and tie it into a bow. The basket is pretty by itself, or it can be used to hold pencils or flowers.

# May Day: May 1

The origin of the celebration of May Day is unclear. Many believe it began in ancient Egypt and India at their spring festivals. It was a favorite holiday for the people of English villages in the Middle Ages. They celebrated by picking spring flowers, choosing a king and queen of May and dancing around a Maypole. This pole was set up in the village square. The people danced around the pole holding ribbons that streamed from the top, weaving the ribbons back and forth until the Maypole was covered with bright colors.

May is a time of the year to be outside and play games of all kinds.

1. Host a May Day olympics in your neighborhood. Play games such as badminton, horseshoes or croquet. Let each family be responsible for a game.

2. Play jump rope with your kids. Get a book, and teach them rope-skipping rhymes. For example:
"Who will I marry?
Rich man, poor man,
Beggar man, thief.
Doctor, lawyer,
Merchant, chief."

3. Make flower piñatas. Kids would enjoy giving one to a friend or to use for May party favors. Blow up a small balloon until it's about 5 inches in diameter; tie it at the neck. Cut newspaper into 1-by-8-inch strips; dip each strip into a bowl of liquid starch. Place wet newspaper strips on balloon until entire surface of balloon is covered, except for a 1-inch square opening around the knot. Let balloon dry. Repeat this process, adding one more layer of newspaper. Allow paper to dry completely. Stick a pin through the opening, pop the balloon, and remove it.

Cut out dozens of 2-inch scalloped circles from various colors of crepe paper. Glue the center of the flowers to the outside of the paper balloon, overlapping the flowers and completely covering the balloon. Pull up the outside edges of each circle to create a flower effect. Fill the flower piñatas with candies and small plastic toys. Seal the hole with a crepe-paper flower. When you give the favor to a friend, tell him or her to crack it open and take out the treats.

4. Make **Flowery Fruit Pizza** for a fun springtime treat. Kids would enjoy decorating this cookie pizza for a party activity.

### Flowery Fruit Pizza

1 17-ounce package sugar cookie dough
1 8-ounce package cream cheese
1 tablespoon milk
2 tablespoons powdered sugar
½ cup red-currant jam
1½ to 2 cups pineapple chunks, maraschino cherries, mandarin orange slices, fresh blueberries and/or sliced strawberries

Preheat oven to 350°. Press sugar cookie dough into the bottom of a 12-inch pizza pan.

Bake 10 to 15 minutes or until golden brown. Cool cookie crust. Mix cream cheese, milk and powdered sugar; spread mixture on crust. Use a selection of your favorite fruits for the pizza topping. Arrange the fruit pieces in flowery designs on top, making sure canned fruit is well drained. Slightly warm the currant jelly in a small pan. Use a pastry brush or spoon to cover fruit with melted jelly. Cut cookie pizza in wedges; serve it immediately or store it in the refrigerator up to 1 hour, uncovered. (Plastic wrap will stick to the fruit.) Serves 6 to 8.

# Mother's Day: Second Sunday in May

In 1907, Anna Jarvis of Philadelphia asked her church to hold a service in memory of all mothers on the anniversary of her mother's death. In 1914, a presidential proclamation designated the second Sunday in May as Mother's Day.

1. Help your kids make a corsage or boutonniere. Encourage family members to carry on the American tradition of wearing a flower today in honor of their mother. Wear a red flower if she is living and a white one if she is deceased. For each corsage or boutonniere you will need:
1 carnation or rosebud
1 piece florist wire (available at craft stores)
1 sprig baby's breath (available at florists)
Green floral tape (available at craft stores)
2 feet of ¼-inch red or white ribbon
1 corsage pin (available at craft stores)
Trim flower stem so that ½ inch remains. Insert florist wire through the thickest part of the stem just below the flower petals. Pull the wire through the stem so that the ends of the wire are even. Twist wire pieces to form a stem; cut wires so they're 2 inches long.

Hold the sprig of baby's breath so that the small blooms form a frame around the back of the flower. Trim the stem to the same length as the wire. While holding the wired flower and baby's breath in one hand, begin wrapping the stems with the green floral tape with the other hand. Start at the top of the stem, slightly stretching the tape as you wind it around the wire to the end. Cut tape off at bottom end of wire, squeezing the end of the tape so that it sticks to the stem. Tie a small bow just under the flower petals with the ribbon. The wrapped-wire stem may be bent into a circle if desired.

2. Plan a mother-daughter luncheon with your daughter. On the invitations, ask each mom and daughter to wear a hat they have made from things found in the kitchen. For example, they can tie wooden spoons on top of an old beach hat or attach a carrot peeler, measuring spoons and other gadgets to an old felt hat. When Judie was ten years old, she and her mother made hats by turning colanders upside down and decorating them with plastic flowers and ribbons. Have a hat style show, and give prizes for the largest, prettiest and funniest hats.

a. When the guests arrive, give them four clothespins or colorful paper clips to attach somewhere on their clothing. During the party, whenever anyone is caught saying the word "you," she must give her clothespin to the person who caught her. At the end of the party, award a prize to the person who has the most clothespins or clips.

b. Play Cotton Ball Chase. Place a dozen cotton balls in front of an empty cereal bowl on a table. Blindfold each guest in turn, and give her a spoon. She will sit in a chair in front of the bowl and, using only one hand and a spoon, try to get as many cotton balls as possible into the bowl in one minute. The person who gets the most balls in the bowl is the winner.

c. Serve finger sandwiches made from pink bread (order from your local bakery) and pink lemonade. Make nut cups from white, 5-ounce paper cups. Line each cup with a 6-inch paper doily, and fill it with nuts and small pastel mints. Tie a thin pastel ribbon around the outside of the cup, making a bow.

3. Have a mother-son Powder Puff baseball game. Invite mothers and sons to come to your backyard or to the park. Choose teams by placing red and blue bandannas in a large paper sack. Ask all guests, without looking, to reach into the sack and pull out a bandanna. They must wear their bandannas during the party to signify whether they are on the red or the blue team. Play baseball with a soft foam ball and a plastic bat. Let the guests take their bandannas home as a party favor.

After the game, give each person a piece of bubble gum, and have a contest to see who can blow the biggest bubble. Award packages of baseball cards to the winning boys and recipe cards to the winning moms.

## Mother's Day Tips for Dads

4. Take the kids to pick out Mother's Day cards for Mom. Allow plenty of time so the kids can pick cards that convey just what they want to say.

5. Make a *Mommy Book* with your preschooler. Help your child cut out pictures from magazines that describe Mommy. Glue the pictures on construction paper, writing a caption for each one. Punch two holes in the sides of the pages, and bind the book with ribbon.

6. Help your kids serve Mom breakfast in bed. Be sure to include a flower in a small vase on her tray. Let the kids sit on the bed while she eats, and take pictures of the occasion. One of Kathy's favorite family photos is of her in rollers, propped up in bed with her children serving her breakfast on Mother's Day. An easy menu might include:

### Broiled Grapefruit

1 grapefruit, cut in half
2 tablespoons sugar-free raspberry jam
1 maraschino cherry

Spread jam on each grapefruit half. Place fruit on small baking sheet. Place grapefruit on bottom shelf, and broil for 3 to 5 minutes until jam is bubbly. Remove grapefruit halves from broiler, and place them on a serving plate. Cut cherry in half, and place each piece in the center of the grapefruit halves.

### Cinnamon Bread Bows

1 can (8 each) refrigerated bread-stick dough
4 tablespoons margarine or butter
2 tablespoons sugar
2 teaspoons cinnamon

Preheat oven to 375°. Unwrap and separate bread sticks. Melt margarine in a shallow pan;

allow it to cool. Dip each bread stick into melted margarine to coat evenly. Carefully form each bread stick into a bow shape, placing them about an inch apart on an ungreased cookie sheet. Combine sugar and cinnamon, and sprinkle it on the bows. Bake bread bows 15 to 20 minutes or until lightly brown. Serve immediately. Makes 8 bread bows.

# Graduation Day

During the last part of May (or first couple of weeks in June), at least one family member or friend usually graduates from something! It might be kindergarten, elementary school, junior high, high school, trade or vocational school, college or graduate school. It's also fun to honor someone for graduating from a tricycle to a bicycle, making it through another year of music lessons, completing a big project, getting a first job or just passing a hard grade at school. Those who meet the requirements of graduation from anything should be honored.

1. Display school pictures of the graduate from previous years. Drape colorful, curly streamers over the pictures to make a pretty centerpiece. (These streamers are available in the party section of most grocery and variety stores.) Decorate your home with crepe paper in school colors, and hang up lots of signs with: Congratulations! You Made It! Write slogans on balloons with the words inside a circle with a slash through them: No School! No Homework! No Report Cards!

2. Frame and hang the diploma. It's an accomplishment to be proud of! Or make a diploma for a family member who has done a special accomplishment that should be honored.

3. Have a picture poster made of the graduate. Just take a good snapshot of him or her to a film processing store.

4. Write a heart-to-heart letter to your graduate with some positive memories you have of him or her. Describe some of the ways he or she has been a blessing in your life. You can also put together a collection of inspirational thoughts. Compile quotations, Proverbs and other Bible verses, wise sayings, sound life principles and uplifting articles. Have copies of your favorite family photos made. Put the letter, photos, articles and sayings in a scrapbook. Present it to a child going away to college or leaving home to pursue a career.

5. Invite the graduate's friends over for a graduation party. Make diploma-like invitations. Let the kids build their own submarine sandwiches. Provide loaves of french bread or submarine sandwich buns, lettuce, tomatoes, sauces, condiments and various kinds of sliced meats, cheeses, green peppers, pickles, olives and onions.

Play the game Who Did It? Pass out an index card and pencil or pen to each person. Ask each person to write down something he or she did in school that no one else knows about. For example, "I played Goldilocks in the third grade play" or "I slipped and fell on the playground while I was trying to impress the girl I had a crush on in fifth grade." The players should not sign their names to the cards. Have one person collect the cards and read them aloud one at a time. The guests try to guess who did it. When the correct person is guessed, he or she must give the details of the incident. Be prepared for some hilarious stories!

# Memorial Day: Last Monday in May

Since the Civil War, this day has been set aside to pray for peace and to honor those who have died in battle while serving our country. In 1948, a presidential proclamation made the last Monday in May the official day.

1. Help your kids make a Stars-and-Stripes candle for a centerpiece. Light the candle, and say a prayer in memory of the men and women who have died in battle while serving our country. Buy one 10-inch white candle; one small square of Styrofoam (to hold candle); red and blue nontoxic, nonflammable slick pen paints. (Check at your craft store for slick pens used to decorate T-shirts.) Place the candle in the Styrofoam square to secure it. Starting ⅔ of the way down, draw straight or squiggly red lines down the sides of the candle to the bottom; draw tiny, blue stars around the top ⅓ of the candle. Allow the candle to dry for 2 hours; then surround it with greenery.

2. Make a Memorial Day wreath to hang on your front door. Cut out the center of a 9-inch paper plate, leaving a 2-inch rim. Staple a 6-inch piece of string to the back of the wreath for a hanger before you decorate it. Cut several 3-inch stars from red, white and blue construction paper. Glue the stars around the wreath, alternating colors, overlapping them slightly.

3. Talk to your children about the privilege of living in America. List some of the blessings we enjoy because men and women have served our country and fought for our freedom.

4. Organize a patriotic kite-flying party. Invite other families to meet at your home to make their own kites. Have kite-making supplies on hand. Decorate the kites in red, white and blue or with patriotic symbols. After making the kites, go to a park or field and fly them. Have a contest to see which kite climbs the highest.

Here's how to make your own kite: you'll need four 36-inch strips of balsa wood ½-inch wide, one 28-by-22-inch piece of craft paper, kite string and two 24-inch strips of 2-inch-wide plastic ribbon for the tail. (These measurements are just a guide; we've made our kites in all different sizes.)

Use scissors to cut one strip of wood 24 inches and a second strip 16 inches. To make the center-cross piece, use a low-temperature glue gun to attach the balsa strips, centering the 16-inch strip 9 inches from the top of the 24-inch strip. Cut two 12½-inch wood strips; join the ends of each strip to the top point of the vertical cross piece and to each end of the crossbar with the glue gun. Cut two 18-inch balsa strips, and glue the ends of each to the crossbar and the bottom point of the cross.

Now lay the wood-strip frame on top of the craft paper; trim it to fit, leaving a 2-inch border. Fold the 2-inch border over the edges of the wood strips; glue the folded edges of the paper to all four sides of the wood frame. Draw stars and stripes on the front of the kite, using tempera paints. Make a small hole in the paper at the center of the cross; thread the kite string through the hole, and tie it to the frame at the cross points. Tie one piece of plastic ribbon to the bottom of the frame for the tail. Cut the second plastic ribbon into six equal lengths; tie one end of each of these strips to the tail ribbon at equal intervals.

5. Serve **Memorial Muffins** and **Stars-and-Stripes Gelatin**. Stick toothpick-size U.S. flags on the top of your favorite muffins.

### Stars-and-Stripes Gelatin

1 6-ounce package blueberry gelatin
1 6-ounce package cherry gelatin

Prepare the blueberry gelatin, using half the amount of water called for. Put gelatin in a 13x9x2-inch pan or dish, and refrigerate it until firm. Prepare the cherry gelatin the same way, putting it into another 13x9x2-inch pan. When the gelatin is firm, cut the blue gelatin into stars, using a star-shaped cookie cutter. Cut the red gelatin into stripes. To serve, place stars and stripes on lettuce leaves.

# Flag Day: June 14

On this day in 1777, Congress adopted the Stars and Stripes as the flag of the United States. Flag Day was officially designated as a holiday by presidential proclamation in 1941.

1. Talk to your children about the importance of honoring the American flag. The United States Flag Code adopted by Congress states, "The flag represents a living country and is itself considered a living thing." Teach children to handle the flag carefully. It should never touch the ground, the floor or water it flies over. Nothing is ever placed on the flag. Clean the flag when it gets soiled, and mend it if it gets torn.[5] The children of one family became so excited about flying the American flag on special days that they began selling flags in their neighborhood.

2. Let your family take part in the national pause for the Pledge of Allegiance on Flag Day. (Check your local library for a copy of the pledge.) At seven in the evening eastern standard time, citizens of the United States are encouraged to participate simultaneously in the Pledge of Allegiance, sharing a patriotic moment together.

3. Help your children make a stars-and-stripes wind sock to hang in your yard. You'll need one piece of 12-by-18-inch blue nylon parachute fabric, one piece of 12-by-18-inch red nylon parachute fabric, three squares of white felt and one ring of a 5-inch embroidery hoop (available at craft stores).

Use a low-temperature glue gun to attach the 18-inch sides of the blue and red material together, allowing a 1-inch overlap with the blue edge on the top side. To make streamers, cut the red material into 1-inch strips starting at the unglued end, cutting to where the blue material meets the red. Glue top part of the blue fabric to the outer rim of the embroidery hoop, overlapping one inch of the blue fabric to make a side seam. Glue the blue side seams together down to where the blue material meets the red. Cut eight to ten 2-inch stars from white felt, and glue them to the blue portion of the wind sock. Cut three pieces of 36-inch white twine. To make a hanger, cut a ⅛-inch slash in the blue material just under the embroidery hoop at three points of equal distance around the hoop. Poke one piece of string through each hole, and tie securely around the fabric and hoop. Tie the three loose end strands of the string about halfway up and again about two inches from the ends. Hang wind sock.

4. Fix these patriotic snacks for a festive treat.

### Red, White and Blue Fruit Flags

4 strawberries or pitted cherries
4 bite-size chunks of apple or banana
8 large blueberries
4 3-inch wooden picks

Sprinkle the apple or banana chunks with lemon juice to prevent them from turning brown. Place 1 strawberry or cherry, 1 apple or banana chunk and 2 blueberries on a wooden pick. Put the fruit picks on a plate, and serve with the following dip. Makes 4 servings.

### Creamy Fruit Dip

3 ounces cream cheese

1 tablespoon milk or cream
1 tablespoon sugar-free strawberry jam

Combine all ingredients in a small bowl, and mix until smooth. Cover bowl; refrigerate dip until ready to serve.

1. William D. Chase, *Chase's Annual Events: Special Days, Weeks & Months in 1989* (Chicago: Contemporary Books, 1989), 67.
2. John W. Wright, ed., *The Universal Almanac 1990* (Kansas City: Andrews & McMeel, 1989), 17.
3. "Don't Trash America!" (Refuse Industry Productions, Inc., 1989).
4. John Javna, *Fifty Simple Things Kids Can Do to Save the Earth* (Kansas City: Andrews & McMeel, 1990), 86.
5. William Hillcourt, *Official Boy Scout Handbook* (Irving, Texas: The Boy Scouts of America, 1979), 418, 422.

# Chapter 4

# Summer Holidays

## First Day of Summer: June

Summer solstice, about June 21, marks the beginning of summer and is the longest day of the year in the Northern Hemisphere. The Arctic Circle experiences daylight for twenty-four hours on this day.

1. Have a sponge war outside using buckets of water and sponges.

2. Make a slippery water slide. Buy a 4½-by-12-foot piece of heavy plastic. Keep the plastic wet with the garden hose while your children slip and slide around. Be sure to put the slide on a soft, grassy area. (Do not attempt to do this on a hard surface. This one requires good safety rules and supervision.)

3. Serve a special summer drink. Dip the rim of a drinking glass in lemon juice and then in sugar. Place glass in freezer for 20 minutes; then

**"And young and old come forth to play On a sunshine holiday."**

*John Milton*

fill it with your favorite beverage.

4. Sit outside on quilts with your kids, and watch the sun set tonight. Enjoy homemade **Frozen Yogurt Pops**. Young children love to make these.

**Frozen Yogurt Pops**

2 cups plain yogurt
1 6-ounce can of frozen orange juice, undiluted
1 teaspoon vanilla

Mix all the ingredients. Pour yogurt mixture into small paper cups; insert ice-cream sticks into the center of each one, and freeze them. Peel away the paper cup to eat the yogurt pops.

## Father's Day: Third Sunday in June

In 1910, Mrs. John Bruce Dodd of Spokane, Washington, started the idea of a Father's Day celebration in her city in the month of June on her father's birthday. She wanted to honor him because of the way he had raised his six children after their mother died young. President Calvin Coolidge publicly supported her idea in 1924. In 1972, it was officially proclaimed a national holiday.

1. Secretly plan your Father's Day activities when Dad is not around. Help your kids make a cardboard crown for him. Cover it with foil. Pick a time to surprise him, and crown him king for the day. Wrap a bathrobe around his shoulders, and give him a bathroom plunger for a scepter. Take a picture of the king and his kids!

2. Help your kids think about Dad by playing a game to see who knows him best. Give each child a piece of paper and pencil. Have them number their papers from one to ten, and ask them to write their answers to ten questions you'll ask. For example: What is Dad's favorite sports team? What is Dad's favorite dessert? What vegetable does Dad dislike the most? If Dad could pick the family vacation spot, where would he go? After all questions are asked, let Dad give the correct answers. Score ten points for each correct answer.

3. Let the kids make gift coupons, listing jobs they'll do for Dad throughout the day. For example, they can fetch his slippers, bring him the paper, fix a snack, pull weeds in the garden or help wash the car. He can redeem his coupons any time that day.

4. Check with your local newspaper about letting the kids place a classified ad in the personal column of the Sunday paper. Help them write a short, encouraging message, such as "We love you, Dad" or "Tom Smith, World's Greatest Dad." See if Dad notices the ad when he reads the paper. Be sure to cut out the ad and save it.

5. Create a handyman's basket for Dad. Fill it with items that are nice to have on hand to fix things around the house, such as Super Glue, a tape measure, duct tape, electrical tape, a small set of screwdrivers and a pair of needle-nose pliers.

6. Let your children help decorate a 13x9x2-inch sheet cake for Dad. Using tubes of colored frosting, decorate a cake with a necktie design on it, a "Go Dad!" pennant or a first-place ribbon.

7. Let your children serve Dad a special hors d'oeuvre before dinner. Help them fix him a plate of crackers, cheese and the following snack.

### Nutty Grape Clusters

3 ounces cream cheese

1 tablespoon cream

1 cup chopped pecans, almonds or walnuts

½ pound red or green seedless grapes

Mix the cream and cream cheese until smooth.

Wash grapes, remove them from their stems, and dry them. Roll each grape in the cream cheese mixture and in the chopped nuts. Form the nut-covered grapes into a cluster on a serving plate. If you have real or artificial grape leaves, they can be placed on top of the cluster for decoration. Serve as a finger food. Makes about 2 cups.

# Independence Day: July 4

This date is the birthday of the United States. In Philadelphia on July 4, 1776, representatives from thirteen British colonies in North America adopted a statement setting forth the reasons for declaring their independence from Great Britain. The draft of the document was largely the work of Thomas Jefferson. The Declaration of Independence proclaims that God gives every person a birthright of life, liberty and the pursuit of happiness. The original document is stored in the National Archives Building in Washington, D.C.

1. Host a neighborhood sidewalk art contest. Ask each child to draw a patriotic picture or symbol of our country, such as a liberty bell, eagle or flag on the sidewalk or driveway. Supply large colored chalk (available at most craft stores). (The chalk will wash off with water; depending on the porousness of the cement, however, you may need to wash it more than once.)

2. Coordinate a neighborhood effort to display 5-by-8-inch flags in every front yard by the mailbox.

3. Organize a neighborhood parade. Help children decorate their tricycles, bicycles and wagons with red, white and blue crepe-paper streamers, balloons and flags. Decorate baby strollers, too. Have everyone dress in red, white and blue. If you do this, be sure to inform your local newspapers or television stations. They're usually looking for a local story like this to cover.

4. Make a pinwheel. Cut a 5-inch square of construction paper; mark the exact center of the square with a dot. Starting at the point of each corner, cut a straight line to within ¼ inch of the dot. Fold every other corner to the center mark, holding each corner with your thumb as you fold the next one over. Push a thumbtack through all the corner points and the center of the paper, and then into the top of a round, 12-inch dowel rod. Allow a little room between the head of the tack and the stick for the pinwheel to spin freely.

5. Attend a concert tonight. Many community orchestras give early evening performances of patriotic music. Or check your newspaper for times and locations of fireworks displays. Take lawn chairs or a quilt to a good viewing spot.

6. Teach your children the words to our national anthem. Make a game by writing out the entire song, leaving out a few of the words. See if they can fill in the blanks. Ask your librarian to help you find a book that has the words to "The Star Spangled Banner," or you might buy a book of patriotic songs for your family to learn together.

7. Prepare this fun frozen dessert with your children.

### Frozen Watermelon Surprise
2 cups lime sherbet
1½ cups pineapple sherbet
2 cups raspberry sherbet
½ cup miniature chocolate chips

Spread 2 cups of slightly softened lime sherbet evenly around the inside of a 6-cup bowl. Place bowl in freezer for 2 hours or until sherbet is firm. Then spread a thin layer of the 1½ cups, softened pineapple sherbet over the lime, freezing it until firm. Mix softened raspberry sherbet with the miniature chocolate chips; spoon this mixture into the bowl of sherbet until it's full. Return bowl to freezer for 4 hours. Unmold sherbet onto a platter, green side showing. Slice it like a watermelon, and serve it on dishes.

8. Invite neighborhood families over to your house, and serve homemade ice-cream pies.

### Ice-Cream Pie
1 quart ice cream (chocolate chip, coffee or your favorite flavor)
1 8-inch (baked or unbaked) graham cracker crust
1½ cups fudge topping
¼ cup pecans or almonds

Firmly press slightly softened ice cream into graham cracker crust. Top ice cream with fudge topping and pecans or almonds. Freeze pie for about 3 hours or until firm. Serves 6.

# First Day of School: August or September

Children across America traditionally start the new school year between August 15 and September 15.

1. Fix your child's favorite breakfast this morning. Judie's granola is always a winner at the Byrd house. Let your children help you make a batch ahead of time. This is a good way to help them learn measurements.

### School Day Granola
½ cup vegetable oil
½ cup honey
1 tablespoon cinnamon
5 cups uncooked old-fashioned oatmeal
1 cup sesame seeds
1 cup sunflower seeds
½ cup wheat germ
½ cup wheat or oat bran
½ cup flaked coconut
½ cup chopped almonds or pecans
1 cup raisins

Preheat oven to 325⁰. Combine vegetable oil, honey and cinnamon in a small saucepan, heating mixture until the honey has melted. Combine the oatmeal, sesame seeds, sunflower seeds, wheat germ, wheat or oat bran, flaked coconut and chopped almonds or pecans in a large bowl. Pour honey mixture over dry ingredients, stirring until evenly coated. Spray a rimmed cookie sheet with nonstick vegetable coating, and spread granola on it. Bake granola for 25 to 30 minutes or until lightly browned, stirring mixture every 10 minutes. After the granola has cooled, stir in raisins, and store it in an airtight container. Yield: 20, ½ cup servings.

2. Have a special prayer at breakfast for your

children's classes and teachers.

3. Take a picture of the kids as they leave the house. The Peels love the first-day-of-school pictures in their family photo albums.

# Labor Day: First Monday in September

On the first Monday in September, we honor the labor force in America. Peter J. McGuire, president of the United Brotherhood of Carpenters and Joiners of America, initiated the idea for Labor Day to celebrate the American worker. The first observance of this holiday included a parade on September 5, 1882, in New York City. It was signed into law on June 28, 1894.[1]

1. Talk to your children about the importance of various occupations and careers. Ask them to think about what would happen if some of the important behind-the-scenes jobs went unfilled. Encourage them to talk about what they would like to do when they grow up.

2. Play Tools of the Trade with your children. Give two clues that describe the tools or equipment used in a specific vocation, for example, seeds and tractor for farmer. Keep giving one clue at a time until the right answer is guessed.

3. Go to a park, build a campfire and have a picnic. Don't let the thought of gathering all the food and gear together make you feel it's not worth the hassle. Getting outdoors is one of the most inexpensive ways to celebrate. You can walk,

fish, go on nature hikes and tell stories around the campfire. We've included the following easy **No-Work Dinners** and a picnic checklist to make your outing a success.

**No-Work Dinners**: Tear off a 20-inch length of heavy-duty aluminum foil. Grease one side with margarine. Break up ¼-pound ground beef into small chunks, and place it on greased foil. Next place a layer of carrots and potatoes, sliced very thin, on the beef. Sprinkle beef and vegetables with half a package of dry onion soup mix, and top with three pats of margarine. Fold foil over the food, and secure it tightly. Then fold over each end tightly so the juices won't run out. Place the foil packet directly on hot coals for 10 minutes. Turn the foil packet over carefully, and cook for another 10 minutes. Unfold foil, and eat right out of it. Make one for each person in your family.

**No-Work Bread**: Buy frozen bread dough at the grocery store. Use 2- to 3-foot green sticks from trees, wrapping about ½ cup of thawed dough around the end of the stick. Hold the stick of bread over the campfire for 10 to 15 minutes or until bread is thoroughly cooked. (Caution: Make sure the sticks are from nonpoisonous trees and are long enough for children to hold their bread over the fire without burning their hands.)

**Baked Apples**: Place a cored apple in the center of a foil square. Put 1 tablespoon margarine or butter, 1 tablespoon brown sugar and 1 teaspoon cinnamon in the center of the apple. Wrap it tightly. Place it directly on the coals for 15 minutes.

**Picnic Checklist**

Do take:

—bug spray.

—your camera.

—bats, balls, hats, outdoor games, croquet or Frisbees.

—a first aid kit.

—a flashlight if you'll be out after dark.

—packaged pre-moistened towels for hands.

—damp paper towels or wash cloths in self-sealing plastic bags for cleanup.

—a tablecloth, beach towel or old quilt to cover the picnic table.

—a large plastic tarpaulin (if there's not a picnic table available) to spread on the ground to protect your quilt or blanket.

—an old sheet or large piece of netting to protect the food from insects while you're involved in activities.

—plastic margarine tubs for each child to collect treasures.

—a one-gallon plastic milk carton filled with water.

—toilet paper if you are in a remote location.

—a large garbage bag to take care of litter. You can line your picnic basket with a trash bag, which will insulate the food, protect it from insects and provide you with a bag at the end of the picnic.

# Grandparents Day: First Sunday in September

In 1979, this day was officially set aside to honor grandparents. It's a day when we help children become aware of the strength, wisdom and guidance of older people. It's also a time for grandparents to show love for their grandchildren. We parents can plan activities that will help bridge the gap between the generations and help our children appreciate their grandparents. Your family can adopt grandparents if yours are deceased or live far away.

1. Let your kids call Grandma and Grandpa today to wish them a happy Grandparents Day. Help your children get to know more about their grandparents by thinking of questions to ask them and then recording the answers in a notebook. For example:

Where did you live when you were growing up?

How many brothers and sisters did you have?

How many different schools did you attend?

What were your favorite things to do when you were a child?

Did you have a pet?

What was the funniest thing that ever happened to you?

2. Write a family newsletter to send to Grandma and Grandpa. Each family member can contribute information about his or her activities.

3. Fill a small picture album with photos of your family, and send it to the grandparents. One family living overseas helped their kids create a book to send. They took photographs of the kids involved in various daily activities, writing descriptive captions under the pictures. This helped the grandparents visualize what their kids and grandkids were doing each day while living on the other side of the world. The book is proudly displayed in their living room.

4. If Grandpa likes to fish, give him a fisherman's gift basket. Line a basket with a blue-and-white checked napkin, and fill it with fishing hooks, lures, a jar of bait, a pair of needle-nose pliers, a roll of fishing line and a bag of the following coating mix for fish.

### Fish Fry Coatin' Mix

1 cup yellow cornmeal

½ cup white flour

1 tablespoon lemon pepper

1 teaspoon onion powder

1 teaspoon garlic powder

1 teaspoon tumeric

1 teaspoon salt

Combine all the ingredients. Pour the coating mix into a self-locking plastic bag. To fry fish, dip it in buttermilk and roll it in the mix. Pour 1 inch of oil into a heavy skillet; then place it over medium heat until oil is hot. Add fish and fry gently for 10 minutes for each 1-inch thickness of fish. Turn fish and brown it on the other side. Remove fish from skillet, and drain it on paper towels.

5. Create a potpourri cottage for grandma. Cut off the bottom 3-inch section of a half-gallon, waxed-paper milk carton. Cut off the slanted roof-shaped top portion of the carton; staple shut the flaps of this top portion to make a roof. Cut 1-by-5-inch strips of paper from brown lunch sacks. Place liquid starch in a shallow bowl. Dip paper strips into the starch, coating them completely. Cover the roof piece and the 3-inch base with the paper strips, allowing them to dry completely. Put a second coat of paper strips on the roof and the base; allow them to dry. Coat the roof with white tacky craft glue, and sprinkle potpourri on it. Apply a second coat of glue and potpourri if necessary to cover roof completely. Allow it to dry. Use lace or rickrack to outline a door and windows on the sides of the house. Glue on buttons, pearl beads or small bows to decorate the house. Fill the base with potpourri, and put the roof on it.

1. John W. Wright, ed., *The Universal Almanac 1990* (Kansas City: Andrews & McMeel, 1989), 15.

# Chapter 5

# Fall Holidays

## First Day of Fall: September

The autumnal equinox, about September 22, marks the first day of fall. The sun rises exactly due east and sets due west everywhere except near the poles. Daylight lasts about twelve hours, eight minutes.[1]

1. Make **Apple Butter** as a family. The Byrds form a family assembly line in their kitchen. Teresa washes, peels and cuts the apples in half. Brian cuts out the cores. Bill and David chop the apples and put them in a kettle. Judie adds the spices and cooks the apples.

### Apple Butter

8 pounds apples (Granny Smith, Jonathan, or other cooking variety)

2 quarts bottled apple juice

3 cups sugar

3 tablespoons cinnamon

1 teaspoon ground cloves

> **"O, it sets my heart a-clickin' like the tickin' of a clock, When the frost is on the punkin and the fodder's in the shock."**

*James Whitcomb Riley*

1 teaspoon ground nutmeg

Wash, peel and core apples. Cut them into fourths. Place apples in a large kettle. Add remaining ingredients, and stir to mix well. Bring to boil; reduce heat. Slowly simmer over low heat until mixture is very thick (about 1-2 hours). Pour hot apple butter into hot sterilized canning jars, leaving about 1 inch headroom at top of each jar. Put lids on the jars, and place them in the freezer after they've cooled. Makes about 6 pints.

2. Make homemade peanut butter with your kids. Place 2 cups roasted, salted peanuts in a blender or food processor. Add 1 tablespoon vegetable oil. Process peanuts until desired smoothness is reached, adding a little oil if needed to make the butter moist.

3. Help children make waxed leaves. Collect

fall leaves, and carefully dip them in melted paraffin wax, laying them out on waxed paper to dry. The kids can create a centerpiece for your table with the leaves and fall vegetables.

4. Have older children ask neighbors to save their old newspapers. Designate a day and time to pick up the papers. Divide the papers into 1-inch stacks, and roll them tightly into paper logs. Tie the logs with raffia. Store the papers by the fireplace to use for starter logs.

5. Plan a football or soccer game tailgate picnic. Invite other families to meet in the parking lot at a certain location before a game. Wear your team colors. Have each family bring a picnic supper for themselves and desserts or snacks to share with the group. To keep young children occupied during the game, bring a few small toys along.

# Columbus Day: October 12

The second Monday in October is a national holiday commemorating the arrival of Christopher Columbus to the New World. On October 12, 1492, after sailing across the Atlantic, Columbus and his crew landed in the Bahamas at the island he named El Salvador. He gave the island natives red caps and strings of beads. Columbus Day was first celebrated in 1792 but was not officially recognized until 1909.

1. Make Indian trading beads from bread dough. Cut and discard the crust from 10 slices of fresh, white bread. Shred the bread slices into a large bowl. Work in enough white school glue to form a soft dough. Shape dough into 1/2-inch beads, one at a time. Store the unused dough in an airtight container to prevent drying. Make a hole through the center of each bead with a toothpick. Spread beads on waxed paper so they don't touch; let them dry overnight. Paint designs on the beads with acrylic paint. After they're dry, string the beads with fishing line to make a necklace.

2. Help your children find Spain on a world map or globe. Read about Columbus, and trace the route he may have traveled from the Mediterranean Sea to the Caribbean Sea.

3. Go on a "Where will we end up?" family adventure in your car. Columbus began a trip not knowing his exact destination, so try the same for fun. Starting at your home, flip a coin each time you stop to see which direction you turn—heads you turn left, and tails you turn right. Set a time limit, and see where you end up. Then take the family to a fun place for dessert.

4. Serve **Cheesy Potato Boats** for dinner tonight. Bake 2 medium-size potatoes until soft. Slice each potato in half lengthwise. Scoop out pulp into a bowl, saving the shells. Mix potato pulp with 4 tablespoons butter, 4 tablespoons sour cream, 1/4 cup grated cheddar cheese and 1 teaspoon salt. Scoop potato mixture back into shells.

Make paper sails, and stick them in the potatoes with toothpicks. You now have the Niña, the Pinta and the Santa Maria, plus one unidentified sailing vessel—probably for the press corps!

# Halloween: October 31

Halloween dates back to the sixth or seventh century. It has long been associated with spirits, witches, ghosts and devils. We find this traditional emphasis undesirable and dangerous for children. They can dress up and enjoy this holiday, however, in many positive, nonviolent ways. At the end of this section, we have included a fun rodeo party kids will enjoy.

1. Start a family tradition of having Dad take the kids to the market to buy pumpkins and help carve funny faces. Take pictures of Dad working with the kids on this project.

2. Roast pumpkin seeds saved from carving pumpkins. Wash seeds in a colander, separating them from the pumpkin fiber and discarding it. Place seeds in a rimmed baking sheet, and sprinkle them with salt. Preheat oven to $325^0$. Roast seeds 20 to 25 minutes, stirring every 5 minutes until they're lightly brown.

3. Have a neighborhood pumpkin painting party for children ages five to ten. Cover your table with brown craft paper or a plastic tablecloth. Supply each child with a small pumpkin and indelible markers. (Be sure they wear old clothes.) When finished, put the pumpkins in a wagon and walk with the children to neighborhood homes to show their pumpkin creations.

4. Organize a neighborhood scarecrow contest. Appoint judges, and ask each neighbor to contribute a small entry fee toward a prize. Have families make and display creative scarecrows in their front yards. The Byrds won a smoked turkey one year for their Superman scarecrow.

5. Let the kids decorate your house with pumpkin apples. Cover apples with orange tissue paper. Gather tissue at the top and secure it with brown string to form a stem.

6. Create a pumpkin brownie with your kids. Prepare a brownie mix as directed on the package. Bake the brownie in a 9x1½-inch or 10x1½-inch round cake pan. Allow the brownie to cool. To make a stem, cut two triangle shapes about 2 inches apart at the top of the brownie. Decorate the brownie with tubes of frosting to make a jack-o-lantern face.

7. Celebrate Halloween in a positive, fun way by having a rodeo party. Invite children to come dressed as cowboys or cowgirls. Give a prize for the best costume. Here are some great activities and fun foods:

a. Barrel Racing Relay: At one end of your yard, place three buckets or chairs in a triangle, leaving them far enough apart so that a child can run between them. This will be your barrel racing course. Let each player ride a stick horse (an ordinary broom will do) from the opposite end of the yard to the barrels, riding around each one and then back to the starting point. Use a watch with a second hand to time each child. The fastest barrel racer wins a prize.

b. Feed Sack Race: Have all the players line up and face the finish line about thirty feet away. Give each player an old pillowcase as the feed sack. Have the players step into the pillowcase with both feet, holding the top of the case with their hands. At the starting signal, the players hop to the finish line.

c. Throw Your Boot in the Ring Race: Make a large circle about five feet in diameter on the grass or floor using a rope, hula hoop or garden hose. Ask the players to take off their shoes or boots and put them in the ring. Have the players line up about twenty feet from the circle. At the starting signal, players run to the ring, find their shoes or boots and put them on. The first one with his or her shoes on runs to the leader to receive a small prize.

d. Make bolo ties. Use 40-inch strips of thin leather or brown shoestrings. Thread each end of the lace through an empty thread spool. Tie knots at the ends of each lace so the spool won't slip off. Bring the leather strip or shoestring over the child's head, pulling the spool up to the neck like a bow tie.

e. Tie gum and candies in red bandannas for the kids to take home as favors.

f. Fix your favorite sweetened powdered drink mix, and call it wrangler water.

g. Serve the following cowhand food at the party:

### Branded Sandwiches

Make your favorite kind of sandwich on whole pieces of white bread. To design a brand, use a heavy piece of paper smaller than the slice of bread, and cut your child's initials or a horseshoe or pumpkin shape. Place the stencil on one side of the sandwich in the center, and sprinkle it with a pinch of cocoa powder. Remove the stencil, and you have a branded sandwich.

### Beef Jerky

1 pound beef flank steak or round steak
¼ cup Worcestershire sauce
1 tablespoon liquid smoke (available in the condiment section with steak sauces)
1 tablespoon salt
1 teaspoon ground black pepper

Trim the fat off the meat, and place trimmed meat in freezer for 20 minutes to make it easier to slice. Slice meat into ⅛-inch strips, cutting with the grain of the meat. Combine Worcestershire sauce, liquid smoke, salt and pepper; add meat, and stir to coat each piece evenly. Cover bowl and place it in the refrigerator for 5 hours or overnight. Then remove meat from the sauce and drain it slightly on paper towels.

Preheat oven to $200^0$. Place cake cooling racks on top of rimmed cookie sheets, and lay pieces of marinated meat across the racks, placing slices just far enough apart so the sides don't touch. Put meat in oven, and cook for 5 to 6 hours until meat is very dark and tough but not brittle. When done, cool meat and store in self-sealing plastic bags. Beef jerky keeps at room temperature for several weeks and can also be stored in the refrigerator for up to 6 months.

### Chocolate Cow Chip Cookies

½ cup cocoa
2 cups sugar
½ cup milk
½ cup margarine

1 teaspoon vanilla
3 cups quick-cooking oatmeal
1 cup chocolate chips
1 cup chopped nuts

Line a rimmed cookie sheet with waxed paper. Mix cocoa, sugar, milk and margarine in a 3-quart saucepan. Bring the mixture to a rolling boil, stirring constantly. Boil 3 minutes. Remove from heat, and add vanilla, oatmeal, chocolate chips and chopped nuts, mixing well. Drop by large spoonfuls (about ¼ cup) onto prepared cookie sheet. Allow cookies to cool 1 hour. Makes about 2 dozen cookies.

# Veterans Day: November 11

Since 1919, Americans have celebrated the signing of the armistice ending World War I on November 11. Originally called Armistice Day, this day became a legal holiday in 1938. In 1954, the name of the holiday was changed to Veterans Day to honor all veterans of our armed services.

1. Let your kids interview a family member or friend who is a veteran of the armed services. Ask questions such as:
What was your responsibility in the service?
Were you ever on active combat duty?
Where were you located?
Where did you sleep, and what did you eat?
How long were you away from home?
What did you learn from your experience?

2. Let your child make a thank-you card and send it to an American veteran. Call your local Veterans' Administration office for names.

3. Decorate your front yard or door today with big yellow ribbon bows. Yellow ribbons signify support and gratitude for those serving in the armed forces away from home and our desire for them to return safely.

4. Have supplies ready for the kids to create patriotic place mats and napkins. Cut white poster board into 18-by-13-inch rectangles for each place mat. Next cut five 1½-by-18-inch strips of red construction paper for each place mat. Glue the red strips horizontally on each rectangle, 1½ inches apart, to make stripes. Cover the mats in clear contact paper, or take them to an office supply shop and have them laminated. Buy dark blue napkins at the grocery store or party supply store. Let the kids paint small stars all over the napkins with a white paint pen. (Be sure to let the napkins dry completely before dinner.) When setting the table, position the napkin horizontally in the upper left corner of the place mat so it looks like a flag.

5. Help your child build a model of an airplane or battleship for a veteran. Kathy's boys built models of the types of World War II airplanes their granddad flew in and then gave the models to him. They learned a lot about history from listening to him talk about the war.

# Hanukkah: November or December

On the twenty-fifth of Kislev on the Jewish calendar, Jewish families all over the world gather with loved ones to celebrate Hanukkah. The holiday commemorates the victory of the Maccabees over the Syrians.[2] When the Temple was cleansed and rededicated after the Syrian desecration, the lamp in the Temple miraculously burned for eight days even though there was oil for only one day. For eight nights, Jewish families celebrate by giving gifts, eating traditional foods and playing games.

1. Make or buy Hanukkah greeting cards, and send them to Jewish friends and neighbors. You can draw or create a six-pointed Star of David on the front of a construction paper card.

2. Rent the movie *Fiddler on the Roof* from a local video store to watch as a family. Talk about the importance of tradition to the Jewish people.

3. Make an edible dreidel. A dreidel is a top that children traditionally spin during Hanukkah. Insert a toothpick through a regular-size marshmallow and then into the flat side of a chocolate kiss-shaped candy. Use the candy dreidels to decorate the tops of cupcakes, or eat them as treats.

4. Make a menorah hand picture. A menorah is a candelabra with eight candles plus one used for lighting the others. Families light these candles for the eight nights of Hanukkah. Trace your child's hands side by side with thumbs overlapping. This is the menorah. Then your child can color it with crayons or markers. Crumple nine small pieces of yellow or orange tissue paper; glue each one on a fingertip to make candle flames.

5. Fix **Bubbie's Latkas.** *Bubbie* is the Jewish word for "grandmother," and latkas are potato pancakes traditionally eaten during Hanukkah.

### Bubbie's Latkas

4 large potatoes
1 small onion
2 large eggs
1 teaspoon salt
⅛ teaspoon pepper
½ teaspoon baking powder
½ cup flour

Grate potatoes and onions. Drain off and discard liquid. Mix potatoes and onions with eggs, salt, pepper, baking powder and flour. Drop by tablespoonsful onto a well-greased, hot griddle or skillet. When the potato pancake is browned on one side, turn it and brown it on the other side. Drain pancakes on a paper towel. Serve immediately with applesauce or sour cream. Makes about 2 dozen.

1. William D. Chase, *Chase's Annual Events: Special Days, Weeks & Months in 1989* (Chicago: Contemporary Books, 1989), 236.
2. John W. Wright, ed., *The Universal Almanac 1990* (Kansas City: Andrews & McMeel, 1989), 17.

| Chapter 6 |
| --- |

# Thanksgiving:
# A Feast of Fun

Thanksgiving, our nation's oldest holiday, is celebrated on the fourth Thursday in November. In the fall of 1621, the Pilgrims and native Indians feasted together to celebrate the harvest and to thank God for plentiful crops. Many of the foods they ate that first Thanksgiving are traditionally prepared today in homes across America. On this day, families gather to give thanks to the Lord for His provisions and for the blessings of the past year.

**"As for the picture-book turkey, the only thing that I share with that animal is a thigh problem!"**

*Erma Bombeck*

be a fun and meaningful holiday. Some families find it helpful to assign parts of the meal to extended family members and friends. That way the host home doesn't have to feel overwhelmed with the burden of cooking for everyone.

To make your preparations as painless as possible, do as much as you can ahead of time so you can enjoy the day. If you like company in the kitchen, make your dinner a family affair. If you

Perhaps the thought of spending hours in the kitchen causes you to wish the Pilgrims had been able to drive through and buy take-home food. Festivity can easily turn into frustration when you feel the need for a special computer program to handle your lists of things to do and cook.

Even so, Thanksgiving doesn't *have* to be a big headache. Whether you enjoy a simple meal with your immediate family or pull out all the stops and spread your table elaborately for many, it can

feel the need for uninterrupted kitchen time, suggest that Dad take the kids on an overnight campout the night before Thanksgiving. One dad did this every year when his kids were growing up. Even though the weather was usually chilly, the kids always looked forward to that time with him.

Whatever your circumstances, remember we all need to take time out, enjoy our family and reflect on our many blessings. The following ideas and recipes will help you create a memorable Thanksgiving for your family.

## Fun Things for Kids to Do

1. Create Pilgrim hats for favors. Cut the bottom out of a 10-ounce paper cup (this will be the top of the hat and will be open). Cover the outside of the cup with black construction paper; glue the paper in place. To make the brim, cut a black circle about ½ inch larger than the widemouthed top of the cup. Center this part of the cup on the brim, and glue them together (this will be the bottom of the hat where the head usually fits, but it will be closed). Cut white paper ½ inch wide to fit the cup for the band; glue it next to the brim. Fill the hats with popcorn for children to eat while you're cooking, or use them as favors at the table.

2. Make Indian corn necklaces. Soak yellow or red dried corn and melon, squash or sunflower seeds in warm water for one hour. Pull softened kernels off corn cobs with your fingers. Use dental floss and an embroidery needle to string the moist kernels, seeds and nuts. Let necklaces dry. (Dried corn is available at grocery or craft stores, and seeds are available at plant nurseries.)

3. Paint Indian faces. Fry fresh corn tortillas in 1 inch oil in a medium skillet until crisp and golden brown. Allow tortillas to cool on paper towels. When the tortillas are cool, paint faces on them with tempera paints. Buckled tortillas add character to the face. Use black yarn for hair, making fringed bangs or braids with the yarn. (Don't eat these tortilla faces.)

4. Design tepees. Let kids color pointed paper drinking cups with designs, using felt-tip markers to make Indian tepees.

5. Create an Indian headdress. Cut a piece of corrugated bulletin board border to fit your child's head; staple it together. Let your child poke feathers into the holes along the top of the border to form a headdress. (Bulletin board border is available at teachers' supply stores, and feathers can be found at craft stores.)

6. Design place mats by cutting brown craft paper or grocery sacks into 13-by-18-inch rectangles. Fringe the edges of all four sides of the paper with scissors. Draw Indian designs on each mat.

7. Make Indian drums by decorating empty oatmeal boxes or ice cream tubs. (Many ice cream shops give these tubs away; be sure to ask for the lid, too.) Paint the containers with dark poster paints. Cut out Indian designs from colored construction paper or form them with thick yarn, and glue them on the sides of the drum.

8. Draw a handprint turkey. Your child can make one by tracing the outline of his or her hand on white paper. Make the thumb into the turkey's head, the fingers into feathers; add feet at the bottom of the palm. Color the turkey with crayons or colored markers.

9. Have younger children make a picture book to show their thanks to God. Fold four pieces of 8½-by-11-inch colored construction paper in half. Staple the folded edges together. Children can draw pictures with crayons or cut out and paste magazine pictures on the pages to show what they are thankful for.

10. Play Scrambled Words. On a piece of paper, print 12 to 15 Thanksgiving words with the letters scrambled. For instance, pilgrim could be *mirlpig*, or turkey could be *reykut*.

11. Create Thanksgiving centerpieces. Let the kids fill a horn-of-plenty basket with fruits and vegetables such as apples, oranges, squashes and gourds. Surround the basket with acorns and fall leaves the kids have collected from the yard.

You can also set out decorative birds, hens or turkeys on the center of the table. Have the kids arrange sprigs of fall greenery, nuts and leaves around the birds.

12. Design a potato wreath with your kids. For each wreath you will need: one 9-inch straw wreath, thirty to thirty-five small, red or white potatoes, box of toothpicks, Spanish moss and a big, decorative bow. Attach the potatoes to the top and sides of the straw wreath with toothpicks; do not cover the back of the wreath. Tuck the moss between the potatoes, filling in all the gaps. Leave a 1 inch gap on the wreath to attach a raffia or bright ribbon bow. This wreath is best displayed lying on the table since it's heavy, or you can prop it on your mantel.

**Making Thanksgiving Memorable**

13. Begin the tradition called Five Kernels of Corn. Place five kernels of corn at each person's place setting. Before the dinner begins, explain to your family and guests that the Pilgrims faced many trials and even starvation. These five kernels represent the hardship and suffering of the Pilgrims and the times when this was all they had to eat. Go around the table and have each person say five things he or she is thankful for, holding up a kernel for each blessing.

14. Have everyone write their blessings in a remembrance book on Thanksgiving day. (Stationary and greeting card stores sell blank journals that would be nice.) Younger children will enjoy dictating what they are thankful for. Each Thanksgiving, read the lists from previous years. It's fun for children to recall what they were thankful for in years past.

15. Before Thanksgiving dinner, ask each person to think of someone who has meant a lot over the past year. When you serve dessert, have the person bring something to the table that symbolizes the one for whom he or she is thankful. Take turns having each person tell about the other significant person and what the particular item symbolizes. For example, a young child might choose a book as a symbol for the teacher who taught him or her to read.

16. Invite a college student or single person over for Thanksgiving. Many people cannot afford to travel long distances to go home. A new family in the neighborhood or a single-parent family might also appreciate an invitation.

17. Hold hands around the table, and say a special prayer at your Thanksgiving feast.

18. Fix a take-out plate of your dinner goodies to deliver to a home-bound neighbor or friend.

**Favorite Thanksgiving Foods**

19. Try this **Pumpkin Soup**, which is a tradi-

tion at the Byrd house. Teresa has the honor each year of serving the soup from a hollowed-out pumpkin.

### Pumpkin Soup

1 large onion
1 large cooking apple
3 cups chicken broth
1 1-pound can pumpkin
1 cup apple cider
¾ cup whipping cream
1 large pumpkin

Chop the onion, and peel, core and chop the apple. In a medium saucepan, simmer the onion and apple in the chicken broth until they're tender. Use a slotted spoon to transfer the cooked onion and apple to a food processor; puree them. Return puree to stock; add canned pumpkin and apple cider. Bring soup to a boil; reduce heat. Simmer soup for 10 to 15 minutes. Add cream and heat until bubbly, stirring frequently. Hollow a pumpkin out, removing pulp and seeds. Pour hot soup into pumpkin and serve. Makes 4 servings.

20. Let kids help make the following simple foods for Thanksgiving:

### Homemade Butter

2 cups heavy whipping cream

Beat the whipping cream with an electric mixer until the cream forms soft lumps. Drain cream through a sieve; discard liquid. Place lumps of butter in a large bowl; mash it with a wooden spoon until it's smooth like soft butter. Add 1 teaspoon salt if desired. Cover butter and refrigerate; it will keep for 1 week.

**Note:** This butter makes dinner rolls much more exciting! Kids love to help and to watch the cream turn to butter.

### Cranberry-Currant-Walnut Sauce

1 12-ounce package of cranberries
1 cup sugar
1 cup red currant preserves or jelly
½ cup water
1 cup chopped walnuts
2 tablespoons grated orange peel

Combine cranberries, sugar, preserves and water in a large saucepan. Bring to a boil; reduce heat. Simmer uncovered for 20 minutes. Remove pan from the heat. Stir in walnuts and orange peel. Refrigerate sauce overnight. Makes 6 cups.

### Cranberry Cheese Pie

1 15-ounce can of sweetened condensed milk
½ cup lemon juice
½ teaspoon vanilla
1 8-ounce package cream cheese
1 16-ounce can cranberry sauce
1 9-inch graham (baked or unbaked) cracker crust

Put condensed milk, lemon juice, vanilla and cream cheese in blender; blend until smooth. Fold cranberry sauce into cheese mixture; spoon filling into the crust. Freeze pie until firm. Remove pie from freezer 10 minutes before serving. Makes 6-8 pieces.

### Hot Cranberry Punch

½ cup brown sugar
1 cup water

½ teaspoon each cinnamon, allspice, cloves, nutmeg
2 16-ounce cans jellied cranberry sauce
3 cups water
4 cups unsweetened pineapple juice

Combine brown sugar, water and spices in a large saucepan. Bring to a boil; reduce heat. Simmer over medium heat until sugar is dissolved. Remove pan from heat; add cranberry sauce, whisking to mix well. Stir in water and pineapple juice. Heat punch before serving. Makes 2 quarts punch.

### Cinnamon Turkey Cookies

1 15-ounce package prepared pie crusts
8 tablespoons granulated sugar
2 tablespoons cinnamon

Preheat oven to 450°. Unfold crusts on waxed paper. Use a turkey cookie cutter to cut out shapes. Roll out leftover scraps, and cut out more cookies. Make "scrap cookies" out of the remaining dough. Combine sugar and cinnamon, and sprinkle it generously on the cookies. Use a metal spatula to transfer the cookies to an ungreased cookie sheet. Bake 8 to 10 minutes or until golden brown. Remove cookies from oven, and allow them to cool on metal cake racks. Makes about 16 cookies.

### Turkey Pocket Pies

1 15-ounce package prepared pie crusts
2 cups cubed, cooked turkey
1 10¾-ounce can cream of chicken soup, undiluted
2 tablespoons milk
½ cup frozen peas
2 tablespoons chopped pimento (optional)
1 tablespoon milk

Preheat oven to 450°. Remove pie crusts from box, and let them sit at room temperature for 10 minutes. Combine undiluted chicken soup, milk, peas and pimento and mix well. Unfold crusts. Spread half of chicken mixture over half of each round of pastry dough, leaving a 1-inch border of dough. Fold uncovered half of dough over chicken mixture, forming a half circle. Pinch edges of dough to form a seal. Prick top of dough in several places with a fork to allow steam to escape.

Place pocket pies on ungreased cookie sheet, and brush tops lightly with milk. Bake for 20 to 25 minutes or until golden brown. Remove pies from oven, and slice each pie in half to serve. Makes 2 large pies or 4 servings.

# Chapter 7

# Overcoming Christmas Chaos

**"I'm dreaming of a quiet Christmas, Unlike any I've ever known; With time to spare in my easy chair, And the children playing calmly at home."**

Christmas is the celebration of the most wonderful gift in all of human history—God sent His Son to earth to redeem our world. The story is incredible, yet simple and beautiful. No wonder people's lives seem to change at this remarkable time of the year!

Our families have discovered that celebrating the birth of Jesus in a memorable way doesn't just happen. Unless preparations are made beforehand, our families are overcome by Christmas chaos rather than the joy and peace we want to fill our homes.

"Plan your work, and work your plan" has become our motto. As simple as it sounds, we must confess we found this out the hard way.

Early in their marriage, the Peels learned it was no fun to rummage through picked-over merchandise. By waiting until the last minute to shop, they set themselves up for a big marital fight one Christmas Eve. On the way to the store, they argued over how much money they could or couldn't spend and what they should or shouldn't buy. With only an hour to shop, they were stressed out, angry and unable to focus on the true meaning of Christmas.

You may also find that the following "Murphy's Holiday Laws" go into effect every December:

1. The time it takes to find a parking place is inversely proportional to the amount of time you have to spend.

2. The more expensive a breakable gift is, the better your chances of dropping it.

3. The other line always moves faster.

4. Unassembled toys will have twice as many screws as you expect, and some will always be left over.

5. Interchangeable parts won't be.

6. All children have built-in detection devices when it comes to finding the Christmas gifts you've so cleverly hidden.

7. Amnesia strikes all family members when the cellophane tape and scissors can't be found.

8. When a broken toy is demonstrated for the store manager, it works perfectly.

9. When you need cash fast, the automatic teller isn't.

10. "Quantities are limited" is always written in fine print.

The following ideas offer practical suggestions and fun activities your family can do to cut down on Christmas chaos during the holiday season.

1. Divide Christmas responsibilities and projects over an entire year. That way, you conquer them without getting stressed out. For example, buy half-price wrapping paper and decorations during the after-Christmas sales. Write down what you purchased on note paper, and clip it to the following December's calendar page so you'll remember what you bought.

2. Make a tentative gift-shopping list in February. Then you can watch for sales during the year. Or plan to have a completely homemade holiday. Begin early and involve the whole family in making handcrafted decorations, cards and gifts.

3. Make jams and jellies for gifts during the summer, when berries are in season. Judie begins to search at this time for interesting containers and jars for jellies and other Christmas goodies. She also grows herbs in her garden for herbed oils and vinegars. These make great Christmas presents for teachers. (See recipes in chapter 11.)

4. Encourage the kids to do odd jobs during the summer to make and save money for Christmas presents. They can also make Christmas gifts to sell. One teenage friend spends a good part of her summer making Christmas crafts; then she has a bazaar at her home during the fall to sell her creations.

5. Bring back a Christmas ornament as a souvenir from your summer vacation. The Byrds look for ornaments at gift shops everywhere they travel. When the tree is trimmed, they're reminded of the fun they had on vacation.

6. Decide in the fall what Christmas goodies you want to cook and give away to friends. In September the Peels decide what Bill will concoct this year. (Kathy says it's no secret who's the best chef in the family.) They watch the newspaper for sales on items that need to be bought in large quantities. All the ingredients are collected and ready for Bill's cooking day in December.

7. Schedule an appointment for a Christmas card photo in October. Update your Christmas card addresses during break time at work or while waiting for car pools.

8. Compose a family Christmas letter to friends, and have it printed in November. This is a great way for long-distance friends and family to keep up with each other. Stuff and stamp the envelopes so they'll be ready to send out the first week of December. Gifts to out-of-town friends and relatives need to be mailed then, too.

9. Decorate for Christmas immediately following Thanksgiving. We like to do this so we can enjoy the festive atmosphere as long as possible.

10. Start a master to-do list on December 1. Check it every morning to see what can be done that day. Cross out the items you have already accomplished, and add any new things that need to be done. Delegate as much as you can to other family members.

11. Make a holiday calendar, and display it where everyone can see it. Record activities and outings so everyone will know what's going on. Check with your child's teacher about the dates for Christmas programs at school. Write down those dates on the calendar early so you won't schedule a conflicting engagement.

12. Look for special Christmas programs, events and outings you can attend as a family. Write the dates on your calendar so you won't miss them. Churches and civic organizations begin to advertise special programs at the end of November.

13. Secure baby-sitters early in the month for social events. Ask the sitter to arrive early enough to allow you some extra time to take a relaxing bubble bath before the event. Send a postcard to the sitter to confirm the date and time. This will prevent a lot of last-minute frustration.

14. Discuss realistic gift expectations with your spouse and children. Talk openly about how much money can be spent, and stick to your budget. Overspending causes stress. One large family we know has found it helps their budget substantially by drawing names among the close members of their extended family.

15. Plan a special kids' shopping day. Set aside an afternoon or evening for Mom to take the kids to buy Dad's present and for Dad to take the kids to buy Mom's present. Give younger children a certain amount of money, and help them choose gifts within their limit. Let older kids spend money they've earned, or help them out by matching every dollar they earn toward presents with one of your own.

16. Stock up on batteries, film and other items you'll need Christmas morning.

17. Set up a gift-wrapping station. Keep boxes, Christmas paper, scissors, tape, and tags in a box, drawer or closet that is easily accessible.

18. Pick a night early in December for the adults to stay up late and wrap presents. We play Christmas music, fix a late-night snack and talk about how excited the kids will be to open their presents.

19. Plan a mother's trade-out week. One mom told us about how she and four other moms pooled their talents and multiplied their time. During the week before Christmas, each mom volunteered to be responsible for entertaining the kids for five hours on one of five days. One mother organized a kids' cooking day. They baked and iced cookies. Another mom planned a day to make inexpensive crafts. Another mother took the kids to a matinee. The kids enjoyed five days of fun, and the moms each had four days to do last-minute shopping and errands.

# Chapter 8

# Fun Family Christmas Activities

Juggling the family schedule at Christmastime can be a challenge for any parent. One year, a calendar full of invitations, activities and outings may sound exciting to your family. The next year, you could be finishing an extremely busy or stressful year. Pulling in from the hectic pace and spending time together in front of the fire may be just what your family needs.

Whether you desire many or fewer holiday activities this year, the following list of ideas will help you plan some memory-making moments for your family.

1. Organize a neighborhood living nativity scene. We know of one neighborhood where the adults helped older kids construct a stable-like shed from scrap lumber and make simple costumes. They advertised by word of mouth. For two hours one night, they played Christmas music while the parents and kids took turns acting the roles of the different characters in the story. The yard was well lit so that observers could see the scene clearly. It was delightful to watch and fun for the participants, too.

2. Host a **Friendship Stew** Christmas-dinner party for families you haven't seen in a long time. Have each guest bring an item from the following list of ingredients for your stew. Start cooking the stew immediately when the guests arrive. Serve **Snowballs** for dessert.

**"At Christmas play and make good cheer, For Christmas comes but once a year."**

*Thomas Tusser*

### Friendship Stew
2 pounds ground beef
4 1-pound cans Italian-style crushed tomatoes
2 medium white or yellow onions
4 large potatoes
1 1-pound can yellow corn
1 1-pound can green beans
1 8¼-ounce can sliced carrots
2 teaspoons salt

1 teaspoon black pepper
1 teaspoon crushed oregano
1 6-ounce package frozen green peas

Brown the ground beef in a medium skillet until no pink is remaining; drain and set the meat aside. Place canned tomatoes in a 4-quart stock pot. Peel and coarsely chop onions and potatoes; add to tomatoes. Add browned beef and remaining ingredients, except for the peas. Bring stew to a boil; reduce heat. Simmer stew slowly for 40 minutes or until potatoes are tender. Add peas and cook 5 minutes longer. Serve the stew with dinner rolls or cornbread. Serves about 8.

**Note**: This is a versatile recipe; it's important to have the canned tomatoes, but if one of the other ingredients is missing, the stew will still be delicious. It can even be made without the meat.

**Snowballs**

Shape any flavor of ice cream into 2- to 3-inch balls, quickly rolling each ball in coconut. Place balls on a cookie sheet and put them in the freezer. To serve, place 1 or 2 snowballs in a bowl. (Put chocolate syrup in the bowl first, if you like.)

3. Open your home to the church youth group for a kids' Christmas party. Play Name That Christmas Song or Saying. Make a list of familiar Christmas songs. Cut pictures, numerals or words from magazines that symbolize titles of songs or phrases from the lyrics. Glue the clues on red or green construction paper in order. For example, you may have the number *seven*, a picture of swans on a lake and another picture of children swimming. The answer to this set of clues would be "seven swans a-swimming." Make a set of twenty to twenty-five songs or sayings. Pass the clues around to the players, and let them write down their guesses to the clues. After every player has had a chance to look at all the clues, read the correct answers. The player with the most correct answers wins a prize.

4. Read Luke 2 aloud from a modern Bible translation. Let the children act out the Christmas story. Help them with props and costumes. A preschooler can play the role of the innkeeper who says, "No room in the inn!" When the Peel children turned kindergarten age, they memorized Luke 2:1-11 and recited the passage to the rest of the family on Christmas Eve.

5. Make an advent candle. Buy a white, 8-inch candle. Starting at the top of the candle, paint twenty-five green-and-red horizontal stripes around the candle using nonflammable, nontoxic acrylic paints. Put the candle in a holder, and surround it with holly and berries. Each night at dinner, starting December 1, decide on something you are thankful for as a family. Let the candle burn down one stripe each night.

6. Purchase a copy of the children's video *'Twas the Fight Before Christmas* for elementary-age children. Watch it together. (*McGee and Me!* videos are available at Christian bookstores).

7. Watch *The Bishop's Wife* and *It's A Wonderful Life*. These old movies are usually available at video stores. Talk about the lessons you learn from the characters.

8. Try to attend a production of *The Nutcracker* and *The Messiah*. If performances are not available in your area, check your local TV listings. They're usually aired in December on public television channels.

9. Study and talk about how people in other countries celebrate Christmas. Incorporate a foreign tradition into your family's usual celebration. You can study about a different country each year and try one of its customs. When one family moved back to America after living in Holland for five years, they brought back the Dutch tradition of having their kids put out a shoe filled with grass on December 5. The traditional story says that Saint Nicholas will ride by that night on a white horse and stop to let his horse eat the grass. If Saint Nicholas learns the children have been good, he'll leave them a treat. If they've been bad, he'll leave sticks. Even though their kids are now teenagers, they continue to practice this fun family tradition.

10. Invite other families to go caroling. Have bells for the children to carry and ring as you walk. Serve hot chocolate with marshmallows, spiced cider and Christmas cookies when you finish.

11. Record a Christmas song or message from your family on an answering machine or tape recorder. One family does this instead of sending Christmas cards. Each member of the family records a short summary of the events in his or her life over the past year; then on Christmas afternoon the kids take turns placing calls to friends whose names and numbers are written on

a list. When the friends answer the phone, the kids simply turn on the tape and play their Christmas greeting.

12. Begin a giant jigsaw puzzle on December 1. See if you can finish it by New Year's Day. The Peels start a different puzzle every year. They keep it out on a table in their family room; when family members have a few extra minutes, they can work a few pieces.

13. Start a special collection for your child. Display it in a prominent place each Christmas. Add one item to the collection every year. You might collect angels, unique Christmas ornaments, nativity sets, Christmas bells or nutcrackers.

14. Ask your preschool child to tell you his or her account of the Christmas story. Record the child's words on paper or with a tape recorder. Let your child draw a picture to accompany the story. Grandma and Grandpa will love receiving this as a present.

15. Let young children invite a few friends over for a birthday party for Jesus. Tell them the Christmas story, using a nativity set. Sing Christmas carols, and have a birthday cake with candles for Jesus.

16. Tape Christmas pictures of friends and family to the side or front of your refrigerator. You will enjoy thinking about them all year long.

17. Read aloud to your family each night during the Christmas season. Year after year we

enjoy reading *God Came Near*, by Max Lucado; *The Christmas Day Kitten*, by James Herriot; *The Christmas Stories of George MacDonald*, by George MacDonald; and *The Best Christmas Pageant Ever*, by Barbara Robinson.

18. Start the tradition of passing the same Christmas gift box between family members. Judie and her sisters have a box that has been passed between them for twenty-five years. Each time a gift is given, the date and the names of the giver and receiver are recorded on the side of the box.

19. Begin a family Christmas journal. Write down the memorable times your family shared: the events you attended, the presents you gave and received and the inevitable catastrophes that happened. You'll laugh about them in years to come.

# Chapter 9

# Deck the Halls and Trim the Tree

A tree trimmed with lovely ornaments, a mantel strewn with holly and ribbon, and a banister adorned with festive garlands help to make the season bright. But the pressure that comes with decorating your house may induce a strong desire to roast the tinsel on an open fire!

Browsing through a December issue of your favorite home magazine can be depressing as well. Just a glance at your own Christmas tree can cause you to wonder how many more of your child's plaster-of-paris ornaments the lower boughs will handle.

Though it sometimes seems impossible, a home filled with the enchanting sights, sounds and smells of Christmas can be created without renting the backdrop to *The Nutcracker* or calling in the string section of the Boston Symphony Orchestra.

For kids, the simple, old-fashioned decorations

**"On Christmas morning, when he [the Velveteen Rabbit] sat wedged in the top of the Boy's stocking, with a sprig of holly between his paws, the effect was charming."**

*Margery Williams*

make the merriest memories of all. Here is a collection of our kids' favorite ways to make our homes festive for the holiday season.

**Festive Decorations**

1. Candy-cane candles: Place two white, 10-inch candles in small squares of Styrofoam to secure them. Use red, nontoxic, nonflammable T-shirt paint to draw stripes in a spiral design down the sides of the candles to make a candy-cane effect. Let painted candles sit in the Styrofoam holders until dry, about two hours. Burn candle as usual. You can also paint other Christmas designs on candles, such as green holly leaves with red berries around the base.

2. Bread bears: Buy frozen bread dough at the grocery store. (One loaf makes one large or two small bears.) Thaw bread; divide and form pieces of dough to make the bear's head, body, arms and

legs. Pinch the parts together to make the bear. Use raisins for eyes and mouth and on the tummy for buttons. Put the bear on a rimmed cookie sheet. Bake the bear at 350° for about 20 minutes or until it's golden brown. Cool bear on the pan for about 10 minutes before removing it to a wire rack to cool completely. Tie a Christmas ribbon around the bear's neck or waist. Place the bear on a mantel, in the center of a table or on a bookshelf.

3. Christmas window scenes: Cover a window with wax glass cleaner; allow it to dry. Let your children draw a scene with their fingers. When the holidays are over, simply wipe the window clean with a cloth, and watch it sparkle.

4. Door mittens: Trace around your child's thumb and fingers on felt to make mittens; then cut them out. Your child can glue sequins, lace and glitter on the mittens. Glue each mitten at the palm to the ends of a 24-inch length of ribbon. Tie the ribbon around the child's bedroom doorknob.

5. Snowflakes: Staple two plastic six-pack drink holders crosswise by the middle strips. Tie white string to the middle of the holders, and hang them from the ceiling.

6. Reindeer door decoration: Turn any size craft broom so that the straws are sticking up. To make a pair of antlers, use red ribbon to tie a few straws at one side of the broom about 2 inches down and make a bow. Do the same with a second piece of red ribbon on the other side of the broom. Cut off 2 inches from the ends of the straws between

the antlers. On the face of the broom, glue on black pom-poms for eyes and a big, red pom-pom for the nose. Tie a big, red bow around the handle at the neck part of the broom. Attach a hanger to the back, and put it on your child's bedroom door.

7. Let older kids make garlands to hang on your tree or across the mantel by stringing popcorn, cranberries, gumdrops or marshmallows. Use dental floss and an embroidery needle for stringing.

8. Candy Christmas tree: Buy a small, Styrofoam, cone-shaped tree at a craft store. Starting at the bottom, use thin metal hairpins or paper clips that have been cut in half to attach individually wrapped peppermint candies all over the tree. Pull the end of the candy wrapper through the loop of the clips or hairpins, pushing the ends of the clips into the Styrofoam. The candies will hang down. Attach a bow at the top of the tree.

9. Pasta garland: Let young children string various kinds of pasta, such as mostaccioli and wagon wheels. Cut a piece of yarn the length needed for the garland. Tie one end of the yarn onto a piece of pasta. Wrap the other end of the yarn with transparent tape, so it's like the end of a shoestring. Alternate different shapes of pasta as you string it. Knot the yarn to the last piece of pasta. The garland can be left natural or spray painted.

10. *Readers' Digest* Christmas Tree: Starting with the first page, fold the top corner down to meet the center crease, making sure the page is

folded sharply. Continue folding all the pages to the center crease. Fold the front and back covers last, using transparent tape to secure them together in a tree formation. Spray it with green, white, gold or silver paint.

11. Dress up favorite stuffed animals with big Christmas bows. Display them on a mantel or shelf. You can also make family collections a part of holiday decorating. For example, tie Christmas ribbon around Sister's dolls, the whistles in Brother's collection or Mom's tea cups. Judie displays her collection of copper cookie cutters.

## Christmas Tree Decorations and Ornaments

12. Make snow for your Christmas tree. Combine 4 cups Ivory Snow flakes with 2 cups hot water. Beat soap and water with an electric mixer until it's thick. Under supervision, let the kids brush soapy snow on the tree with their hands. You can also put the snow in the corners of your windows to create a white-Christmas, snowbank effect.

13. Ice-cream stick reindeer: Glue two ice-cream sticks together at one end, forming a V-shape. Glue another ice-cream stick 1 inch down and across the open ends of the sticks. The two points sticking up are the antlers. Glue a red pom-pom at the point of the V-shape for the nose and a black pom-pom in the middle of each stick for eyes. Tie a string at the top crossbar to hang it.

14. Cinnamon stick ornaments: Use a hot glue gun to glue six or seven cinnamon sticks together in a small bundle. (An adult will need to help with

this.) Tie a red ribbon around the middle of the bundle, leaving enough to make a loop for hanging. Stick a small sprig of holly or greenery under the tied part of the ribbon.

15. Three-dimensional ornaments: Use Christmas cookie cutters to trace patterns onto old Christmas cards. Cut out two identical shapes to make each ornament. Cut a vertical slit from the bottom of one shape to the middle point. On the second shape, cut a slit from the top down to the middle point. Slide the two shapes together to make a three-dimensional ornament. Glue glitter on it, or decorate it with colored markers. To hang the ornament, glue a loop of thin ribbon or yarn at the top.

16. Lace balloons: Blow up small, round balloons, and tie them at the neck. Soak a ball of heavy string in liquid starch. Wrap the string around the entire balloon in different directions, leaving a gap to remove the balloon. Let it dry overnight. Puncture the balloon, and gently remove it from the lace-like form. Hang it with thread or a ribbon.

17. Walnut strawberry ornament: Paint a large walnut with red acrylic paint. After it's dry, form a loop out of a 4-inch piece of thin, gold cord or ribbon, attaching the ends to the top of the shell with a hot glue gun. From a 1½-inch square of green felt, cut a four-pointed star. Make a small hole in the center of the felt star, and slip it over the cord. Secure the felt star to the top of the walnut with glue. Use white tacky craft glue and tweezers to glue tiny, black beads on the walnut for strawberry seeds.

18. Potpourri ornament: Cover a 3- or 4-inch Styrofoam ball with white school glue. Then roll the ball in potpourri. Add more glue and potpourri until the ball is completely covered. Place it on waxed paper to dry. Tie a pretty ribbon or lace around the ball, making a hanger by forming a loop and securing it with a floral pin.

19. Pasta snowflake: Create a snowflake design with wagon wheel macaroni. Glue the edges of several macaroni together with a hot glue gun or white school glue to make the snowflake; put it on waxed paper to dry. The snowflake can be left natural or sprayed with metallic paint. Hang the snowflake with ribbon or yarn.

20. Popcorn balls: Form 3-inch popcorn balls, and cover them with squares of pastel-colored plastic wrap. Tie a ribbon around the gathered top of the wrap, and form a hanger. One friend's children covered their tree exclusively with these ornaments. You can also keep these balls in a big bowl or basket near your front door for children to hand out to visiting friends.

### Popcorn Balls
5 quarts popped corn
4 cups sugar
2 teaspoons salt
1 cup water
2 tablespoons butter
¼ teaspoon cream of tartar

Place popped corn in a large bowl. Mix the sugar, salt, water, butter and cream of tarter in a medium saucepan; bring it to a boil. Cook syrup to firm ball stage (245°). Pour syrup over the popcorn, stirring gently to coat the kernels. But-

ter hands, and quickly shape popcorn into 3-inch balls. Makes 20 balls.

21. Cinnamon spice ornaments: Mix ¾ cup ground cinnamon, 1 tablespoon allspice, 2 tablespoons ground cloves, 1 tablespoon nutmeg, and 1 cup applesauce in a small bowl. Pat out the spice mixture onto waxed paper to a ⅜-inch thickness. Cut out shapes using cookie cutters. Peel away excess dough. Make a hole in the top of each ornament with a toothpick. Let ornament dry on waxed paper, uncovered for four or five days. Thread ribbon through the hole, and make a hanger. (If edges of the ornament are rough, smooth them with an emery board.) These ornaments have a great fragrance.

22. Victorian ornament: Cover a pointed paper cup with a round paper doily. Staple or glue the doily to the cup securely. Staple a pipe cleaner at the top of the cup on opposite sides to form a handle. Fill the cup with treats, and hang it on the tree.

23. Christmas cookie ornaments. Use a wooden pick to form a hole in the top of gingerbread or sugar cookies as soon as they come out of the oven. Thread thin red or green ribbon through the hole; tie the ends together to make a hanger. Decorate the cookies with **Royal Glue Icing.** (See chapter 10, number 26.)

## 7 Easy Wreaths
24. Popcorn and teddy bear wreath: Use a low-temperature glue gun to cover a 10-inch Styrofoam wreath with about 2 quarts of popped popcorn. (Stale popcorn works best.) Glue small

teddy bear cookies or other animal crackers, candy canes, red lollipops or various candies onto the popcorn. Insert a wire hanger at the back of the wreath.

25. Ribbon bow wreath: Use pretty plaid Christmas ribbon to make dozens of 3-inch-wide bows. Use floral pins to attach the bows to a 10-inch Styrofoam wreath form, covering it completely.

26. Family wreath: Attach family memorabilia to a 12-inch straw wreath. Choose items that represent the hobbies and interests of each family member, using school pictures, small, wooden initials and tiny toys. Put a big red bow at the bottom of the wreath.

27. Cowboy wreath: Tie a raffia bow around a small child's cowboy boot. Use a hot glue gun to attach the boot to a straw wreath to one side in the front and at a slight angle. Let your children arrange a variety of dried flowers or wheat in the boot. Wrap a red bandanna around the top of the wreath for hanging.

28. Spackle sculptured wreath: Mix 1 cup water with 1 cup spackle (available at hardware stores) until it forms the consistency of whipped cream. Mix in green food coloring. Spoon colored spackle onto waxed paper, and mold it with your hands or the back of a spoon into a wreath shape. (You can also mix in the food coloring while molding the wreath.) Allow the wreath to dry about two hours. Tie a big, red bow around the bottom of the wreath; display it on a shelf or mantel.

29. Holly handprint wreath: Cut the center out of a 9-inch paper plate so that only the rim remains. Help your child trace his or her hands on green construction paper about fifteen times; cut out the prints. Glue the palm of the hands to the inner rim of the ring, the fingers pointing out. Cut small, red circles for berries from construction paper. Glue clusters of three berries on the handprints around the wreath. Punch a hole in the top of the plate, and hang it with yarn.

30. Gumdrop wreath: Cover a 6-inch Styrofoam wreath with gumdrops, using toothpicks that have been cut in half. Hang the wreath with a red ribbon.

**More Festive Ideas**

31. Sugared fruit centerpiece: Wash and dry apples, pears, red grapes, plums or other fruit. Dip fruit into beaten egg whites; then roll the fruit in granulated sugar. Let your child arrange them on a pretty tray or in a bowl. (This fruit is edible if eaten on the day it's made.)

32. On the last day of school before Christmas vacation, put red and green balloons on the mailbox to welcome your children home.

33. Tie plaid ribbons or bandannas around your dog or cat's neck to include them in your holiday celebration. You can even tie a pretty bow on your aquarium or bird cage.

34. Shine red and green apples with a cloth, and put them in a bowl for a simple but elegant centerpiece. The Peels' youngest son enjoys eating a piece of the centerpiece each day. He also gets

to rearrange the apples after he has eaten one.

35. Make pretty Christmas baskets. Use a hot glue gun to attach decorative moss around the rim of a medium-size basket. Then glue red berries and small pine cones on top of the moss. Use this attractive basket to hold Christmas cards or potpourri.

36. Golden artichoke candle holders: Cut out the center of fresh artichokes. Spray the remaining leaves with gold spray paint. Place a votive candle in a glass holder in the artichoke.

37. Luminarias: Have your kids cut out Christmas shapes from the sides of plain paper bags. Leave at least a one-inch base without holes at the bottom. Put about one inch of sand in the bottom of the bag. Place a votive candle in the middle of the sand. Use these luminarias at night to light your driveway or the walkway to your front door. (Be careful: they are highly flammable.)

38. Fruit or vegetable candle holders: Carve a hole down the center of an apple, orange, winter squash or small pumpkin to make a candle holder. Make sure it fits the base of a candle. Holding holly or other greenery at the base of a candle, insert them together into the hole of the fruit or vegetable; make sure they fit snugly. Tie thin gold cord around the candle and greenery.

39. Simmering scent: Put a chopped apple and the peelings from an orange into a small pan of water. Add a cinnamon stick, several whole cloves and a teaspoon of nutmeg and allspice. Bring the mixture to a boil; reduce heat. Simmer slowly until the wonderful, spicy aroma fills your home. Replace water as needed.

40. Christmas ball candle holders: Pull the hanger out of a glass Christmas ball ornament. Glue a household washer to the bottom of the ball to keep it from rolling. Use a funnel to pour about two tablespoons of sand into the ball. Insert a thin candle into the hole. Tie a slender ribbon around the neck of the ball, making a bow. Then place the candle holders on a square mirror tile (available at hardware stores). (Be careful if a ball breaks; the pieces are very sharp.)

41. Cookie tree: Cover a 24-inch Styrofoam cone with 2-inch-wide, plaid Christmas ribbon. Start at the top of the cone, and wind the ribbon around it until it's completely covered; use straight pins or a hot glue gun at various spots to secure the ends and sides of the ribbon. The ribbon will form small pleats and folds, which will add softness to the look of your tree. Glue or pin a bow at the top of your tree.

Bake your favorite sugar cookies in 2-inch designs. As soon as they come out of the oven, use a wooden pick to form a hole at the top of each cookie for hanging. Cool and decorate cookies. For hangers insert toothpicks through the ribbons into the Styrofoam cone at 3-inch intervals, leaving half of each toothpick sticking out. Place the tree on a large serving platter. Then let the children hang the cookies on the toothpicks. Surround the tree with extra cookies.

42. Display family Christmas pictures from years past in a special photo album or in a location where everyone can enjoy them at their

leisure. The Peels tape twenty years of Christmas photos in chronological order to a wall in their family room.

43. At the end of the season, cut your Christmas tree branches into hand-size sprigs, and place them in a wicker basket by the fireplace. Throw a few bunches into the flames every now and then to produce a wonderful fragrance.

# Chapter 10

# Better Busy Than Bored: Fun Projects for Kids

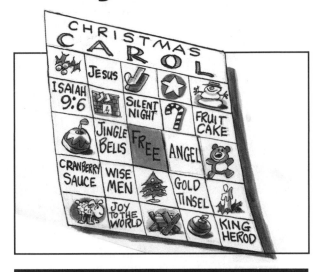

There's something about Christmas in the air that stirs the creative juices of children. Little ones are as pleased as punch just to see their holiday artwork displayed on the refrigerator. They love contributing their masterpieces to the family celebration. Older kids get excited about creating handmade gifts for friends and family members, while some kids just need a healthy diversion from a steady diet of TV.

It's easy to feel as if you'll need a bank loan when your kids cry the words "I'm bored!" But we've listed many projects that are inexpensive and easy to do. Some of these activities will even buy you time to slip back into the bedroom and wrap a few packages while the kids are involved in their projects. You'll also find great ideas for gifts that kids can make.

Furthermore, getting kids involved in something creative can be a great way for them to expend some of that excess holiday energy, which they all seem to have in abundance! With those goals in mind, try the following activities.

**" 'Twas the week before Christmas and all through the house, the children were bored; I cried 'Help!' to my spouse. He said, 'Get out the art supplies, paint, glue and twine. Let's keep them all busy for your sake and mine!' "**

**Younger Children**

1. Make a fireplace from a large appliance box. Cut an opening for the hearth large enough for your child to climb in and out of. Help your child cover the box with brick-like contact paper, or paint brick designs on it with acrylic paint. You can even make stockings from old socks for your play fireplace. The children will love pretending to be Santa coming out of the chimney. (Caution children not to play in a real fireplace or try to start a fire in their pretend one.)

2. Paper reindeer: Help your child trace around his or her shoe on light brown construction paper; cut out the shape. This will be the reindeer's head.

Trace around both your child's hands on dark brown construction paper; cut out the handprints. Glue the hand shapes to the heel of the shoe shape to form the antlers. Glue on black circles for eyes and a red pom-pom nose.

3. Tie small bells on your child's tennis shoes with red or green ribbon. Kathy says it's fun for Mom to do this, too, but be prepared to sing more than a few rounds of "Jingle Bells" every day.

4. Cover your kitchen table with butcher paper. Let your child draw red and green designs all over the paper. Use it as a tablecloth for dinner one night.

5. Wet chalk drawings: Draw snowmen on red or green construction paper with chalk that you continue dipping into a glass of water. Or lightly wet the paper, and draw with dry chalk.

6. Count the days until Christmas. Tape a December calendar page to the front of your refrigerator, low enough for your preschooler to reach it. Every day he or she can color in a square and count the days remaining until Christmas.

7. Have a sugar-plum tea party for your daughter and her friends.

### Sugar Plums

1 cup chopped, dried fruits (apricots, apples, dates or mixed fruits)
¾ cup chopped nuts and/or coconut
2 tablespoons orange juice or maple syrup
Granulated sugar

Combine fruits, nuts and/or coconut and juice or syrup until well mixed. Form fruit mixture into 1-inch balls; then roll the balls in sugar. Cover fruit, and store it in the refrigerator for up to 6 weeks. Makes about 2 dozen.

8. Play Name That Tune. Partially fill eight glasses with varying amounts of water to make a musical scale. Tap the glasses with a spoon to play simple Christmas songs. Let your child guess what song you're playing.

9. Act out the Christmas story. Fill a large box or basket with costumes and props. Old pillow-cases and dish towels secured with elastic head-bands work well for shepherds. Gabriel's outfit can be created from an old sheet with a scarf at the waist and wings made from white cardboard. Make crowns for the wise men from poster board and glitter or sequins. Decorate old shoe boxes with gold paper to be the wise men's gifts. If your kids want to have a beard, apply a thin coat of cold cream before drawing on a beard with an eyebrow pencil. (It will then wash off easier.)

10. Draw a Christmas picture or design on paper using crayons. Paint over the picture with watercolors, covering the entire sheet. Only the areas without crayon will absorb the paint, making an interesting effect.

11. Refrigerator magnet Christmas tree: Use metal lids with rimmed edges (not the kind with sharp edges) from about twenty frozen juice cans. Cut a round piece of green felt to fit inside the rimmed edge of eleven of the lids; cut several different bright-colored pieces of felt to fit inside the remaining lids. Glue the felt to the lids. Attach

a rubber-type magnet to the back of each lid. Your preschooler will enjoy creating a Christmas tree with lights on the front of your refrigerator with the magnets.

12. Tape three different-colored crayons together, and draw on white wrapping paper. Young children will love wrapping a present using their original paper.

**Fun Things to Do with Last Year's Christmas Cards**

13. Make Christmas place mats. Cut out pretty pictures and scenes from cards, and completely cover a 13-by-18-inch piece of poster board. Then cover both sides with clear contact paper.

14. Create gift tags and postcards. Cut out pictures from Christmas cards; use the back side to write your message.

15. Let your children decorate their rooms with the cards. Stick them on walls and mirrors with picture-mounting putty. (It's available at most office supply stores and does not take paint off walls.)

16. Christmas felt board: Cover a 24-by-24-inch piece of sturdy cardboard with white felt. Cut out a 20-inch Christmas tree shape from green felt. Glue a small strip of Velcro to the back of small Christmas card pictures you've cut out, and decorate your felt tree with the pictures. You can also create stories and design scenes on the felt board with the Christmas card pictures.

17. Let your child cut out artwork and messages from last year's cards to decorate this year's packages; glue the cards on the paper after the gift is wrapped.

18. Christmas shadowbox: Cut out similar pictures from Christmas cards, such as all snowmen, nativity scenes or Santas. Glue the pictures to the back and bottom of a shallow gift box to make a collage. Pictures of angels can be hung with string from the inside top of the box. Spray paint shell-shaped macaroni gold; then glue it around the inside edges of the box to frame your collage. Or you can glue pretty lace around the inside edges of the box.

19. Christmas diorama: Cover a shoe box and lid with Christmas paper. Cut a 2-by-4-inch opening in one end of the box. Cut double doors at the other end. Cut a 1-by-2-inch opening near one end of the lid of the box. Make a scene by cutting out small, Christmas-card figures with a 1/8-inch fold at the bottom of each one. Tape the figures standing up to the inside bottom of the box in staggering locations and facing the double doors. Tape a piece of red cellophane inside the lid over the opening and inside the box over the 2-by-4-inch opening. Put the lid on the box with the two cellophane openings nearest to each other. Look through the double door end of the box to view the scene. It's enchanting!

20. Mosaic bank: Use white school glue to completely cover an empty jelly jar with small pictures from cards. When the pictures are dry, apply a coat of clear acrylic paint. Punch an oval-shaped hole in the lid to insert coins. Have each family member deposit pocket change each day

during the month of December. Then go as a family to donate this money to a church or organization that helps needy families at Christmas.

### Older Children

21. Christmas Carol Bingo: Make bingo-type cards using the word *CAROL*. Make a list of fifty Christmas terms, songs or items. Draw pictures or write words for those fifty items. Designate ten pictures or words for each letter in *CAROL*. For example, the *C* may include: Carols, Mary, cards, chimney, decorations, gifts, lights, ornaments, wreath and wise men. For each card, put five of the ten pictures or words under each letter, varying their position on each card. Put each of the fifty terms or pictures on separate cards for the caller to use, such as *A, stocking*; *C, toys* or *L, tree*. To play bingo, draw a card from the stack, call the name of the item, and let the players cover up the word or picture on their cards with a penny or bean. Continue calling items until the first person has all the items across, down or diagonally and calls out "Christmas Carol." Give small prizes such as candy to the winners.

22. Caulk art: Use a 6-ounce tube of latex caulk to draw Christmas scenes or designs on cardboard, forming a raised effect. When the caulking is dry, paint it as desired with acrylic paints. Or use dark-colored cardboard, and leave the caulk white to create a winter snow scene.

23. Goodies swap: Allow an older child to invite friends over for a holiday goodies swap. Ask each guest to bring one dozen homemade cookies for each person invited, plus one extra dozen. For example, if five kids are invited, they should each bring six dozen cookies. Place each child's extra dozen on trays for everyone to eat at the party. Display the remaining cookies, and let the kids choose assorted cookies to take home. If five kids come, they'll have five dozen cookies to take home or give away for Christmas gifts.

24. Create a Christmas tree for the birds. Choose a tree in your yard to decorate. String popcorn, cranberries, raisins and apple slices on fishing line. Make edible ornaments for the birds' tree from Christmas cookies you overcooked. Coat them with lard, and dip them in birdseed. Tie string around the cookies, and hang them on the tree. (After the food has been eaten, remove the fishing line so the birds won't get tangled in it.)

25. Paint sugar cookies. Let your children make your favorite sugar cookie recipe, using cutters to make Christmas shapes. Then paint Christmas designs on the cookies. Make paint by mixing one egg yolk with ¼ teaspoon water. Add a few drops of food coloring. Brush paint on cookies before baking them.

It's also fun to make and paint sugar cookie dough sculptures. Let your children form animals, snowmen or other sculptures from cookie dough. The kids can bake and eat their masterpieces. You'll need to bake high-density cookie sculptures longer.

26. Graham cracker house: Break four large graham crackers into halves to make eight pieces. Using a serrated knife, cut one square diagonally to make two triangles. Using the **Royal Glue**

Icing recipe below, connect four squares for the sides of the house. To make the roof, glue two squares at a slant, fitting them to the two triangle pieces to make the front and back of the roof. Glue the roof to the house. Decorate the house with gumdrops, peppermints and other candies. You can also stack cinnamon sticks at the side of the house to look like logs. Make grass to spread around the house by dying shredded coconut with green food coloring.

### Royal Glue Icing

1 large egg white
1½ cups sifted powdered sugar

Beat the egg whites and powdered sugar until the icing is somewhat fluffy and has the consistency of thick glue. If icing is too thin, add more powdered sugar. If it's too thick, add a few drops of water. Store the glue icing in an airtight container.

27. Crayon printing: Draw a Christmas picture or message on a 4-by-6-inch piece of heavy paper with a thick coating of crayon, but write the message backward. Lay a piece of paper on an ironing board to protect it; then lay on top of the paper an 8-inch square of white muslin and the picture with the colored side facing the fabric. (Make sure the picture is in the center of the fabric square.) Place another piece of paper over the crayon design. Iron over the paper cover with a warm iron, holding it on top of the paper for about three seconds. Remove the cover paper and the colored one to see your print. Frame the muslin picture in an embroidery hoop large enough to fit the design.

28. Catalog scavenger hunt: Save the multitudes of Christmas catalogs you receive in the mail, and make a list of specific household items and toys in them. Give each participant a pair of scissors, and set the kitchen timer for twenty minutes. See how many of the items they can find and cut out in that time. The one with the most pictures gets a small treat.

### Fun Gifts Kids Can Make

29. Jeweled picture frame: Use a hot glue gun to cover inexpensive picture frames with old jewelry pieces. Use earrings, bracelets, old watches, charms and other interesting pieces. A 4-by-6-inch frame works best, since a larger frame may become too heavy.

30. Sewing ribbon: Cut a piece of 1-inch-wide grosgrain ribbon 48 inches long. Tie one end to one handle of a small pair of sewing scissors. To the other end of the ribbon, attach a lightweight pin cushion. The ribbon hangs around your neck. Give this gift to someone who sews or does stitchery.

31. Orange pomander: As you poke holes in an orange with a large darning needle, push a whole clove into each one. Cover the orange with cloves in rows or in a random pattern. In a self-sealing plastic bag, mix 2 tablespoons each of ground cinnamon, cloves, nutmeg and orris root. (Orris root is a preservative and is available at craft stores or where potpourri supplies are sold.) Roll clove-studded fruit in the spice mixture until it's heavily coated. Remove orange from the bag, leaving a thin coat of spices on the fruit. Allow the orange to dry for three weeks. The fruit will become dark and hard. Give it as a gift with in-

structions that the fruit is preserved and will last indefinitely. The scent of the pomander may be refreshened with a few drops of potpourri oil. Display the orange in a bowl all year.

32. Christmas wreath earrings: You will need two 12-inch, green pipe cleaners, tiny colored craft beads, four 4-inch strips of red string and two earring clips. Form a 1½-inch circle with a pipe cleaner, wrapping it around itself. Tuck the ends of the pipe cleaner into the twisted wires so they're hidden. Attach an earring clip to the top back part of the circle. Tie two small pieces of red cord into a single bow. Glue the bow onto the front, top of the wreath shape; then glue tiny beads all over it. Do the same for the second wreath.

33. Animal cracker pins: Coat an animal cracker with varnish three times. Let it dry thoroughly between each coat. When the third coat is dry, glue on a pin backing. (These are available at craft stores.)

34. Stenciled welcome mats: Obtain a rectangular carpet sample from a carpet store. Buy stencils at a craft store, or make your own by drawing designs on thin cardboard; then cut out the shapes. Use Christmas symbols, the word *Welcome* or the recipient's last name for stencils. Place the pattern on the carpet sample, and brush on acrylic paint. Carefully remove the stencil; allow the paint to dry.

35. Milk carton ice candles: Wash and dry a pint-size milk carton. Cut off the flaps. Lightly coat the inside of the carton with cooking oil.

Make a small hole in the bottom of the carton with the point of scissors. Tie a 10-inch piece of twine or cotton wick (available at craft stores) to a pencil, which will rest on top of the carton. Thread the other end of the twine through the inside of the carton. Pull the string taut from the outside bottom of the carton, and tie a knot to secure the wick in place. Next melt paraffin in the top of a double boiler. You can add food coloring to the melted wax if desired. (When the candle hardens, the color will lighten.) Fill the milk carton with ice cubes; then carefully pour the melted wax into the milk carton. Allow the candle to cool for about two hours or until completely hardened. Unmold the candle over the sink so that the water from the melted ice cubes goes down the drain. Gently tear off the sides of the carton. Trim the twine (attached to the pencil) to candlewick length. The candle will be filled with interesting holes and tunnels where the ice cubes once were. (*Warning: hot wax can be dangerous. This activity should be closely supervised by an adult.*)

36. Christmas necklace: Buy a 2-inch metal bell at a craft store. Thread a 24-inch piece of 1-inch red or green grosgrain ribbon through the loop at the top of the bell. Tie the ribbon, and wear it as a necklace. This is a nice gift that your daughter can make and give to her friends.

37. Potpourri: Collect leaves, pinecones, pine needles and/or dried flowers. Put them in a quart-size, self-sealing plastic bag with cinnamon oil; put the bag in the freezer for two days. This sets the scent. (Cinnamon oil and other potpourri fragrances are available at craft stores.)

38. Doorknob signs: Older children will enjoy making these signs (similar to the ones found at hotels) for their friends. Cut out a 3½-by-8-inch rectangle from cardboard. Measure down 1½ inches from one end of the cardboard, and draw a 2½-inch circle in the center. Cut out the circle and a 1-inch bump at the top of the circle, where the sign will rest on the doorknob. Personalize the sign on one side: for example, *David's Room.* Write *Do Not Disturb* on the other side. Decorate the hanger with stickers, paint pens or colored markers. Cover it with clear contact paper.

39. Recipe file: Buy an inexpensive, 3-by-5-inch card file. Help your kids cover it with self-stick fabric (available at variety or craft stores). Let them choose their favorite recipes; then copy them onto 3-by-5-inch index cards. Use divider cards (found at stores that carry kitchen supplies), for different categories of recipes. Give the file to a friend who likes to cook.

40. Create a terrarium. Use a wide-mouth, 1-gallon glass jar. First place 1 inch of small gravel or pebbles in the bottom of the jar. Then spread a 1-inch layer of sand over the gravel. Make a third layer of equal amounts of potting soil and peat moss 2 inches deep. Place small plants in the potting soil. Decorate with rocks or shells. Punch several holes in the lid, and screw it on. Send instructions to mist the plants about once a month. If moisture clings to the side of the jar, the terrarium has enough water.

41. Make a pretty waste basket. Spray paint a plain wicker waste basket with white or a pastel color. Attach silk flowers and grosgrain ribbon bows around the basket with a low-temperature glue gun.

42. Make a berry container into a ribbon spice basket. Cut three 24-inch lengths of ½-inch-wide ribbon. Weave ribbons into the plastic berry container, tying the ends of the ribbons into bows. Fill the basket with a bottle of whole cloves, cinnamon sticks, a few whole nutmegs and a nutmeg grater.

43. Button picture frame: Use a hot glue gun to attach old buttons of various sizes, shapes and colors to the top part of a 1-quart canning jar ring. Glue two 1-inch buttons close together to one side of the rim to form a stand. Using the flat lid for a pattern, cut out a photograph to fit inside the ring. Place the photograph and lid inside the ring frame, securing the lid in place with a few spots of hot glue.

44. Bracelets: Thread a 12-inch length of heavy elastic thread through the holes of various colors and sizes of buttons that are ⅝ inch or larger. Check to make sure the elastic will go through the holes. Thread the elastic through one hole of each button. You'll need about forty-five buttons. When all the buttons are threaded onto the elastic, adjust the elastic so the bracelet is comfortable around the wrist. Then thread both ends of the elastic through the holes of one button, knotting the elastic at the ends.

45. Earrings: Stack two or three buttons of staggering sizes, the largest at the bottom. Use a low-temperature glue gun to join the buttons. When the stack is dry, glue it to the ear clip. (Buy ear

clips at a craft store.)

46. Barrette: Use a low-temperature glue gun to attach various-size buttons to the barrette. You'll need eight to ten buttons. (Purchase a barrette form from a craft store.) Girls love to make and give these to their friends.

# Chapter 11

# Fun with Festive Foods

Most of us bring at least one tradition from childhood into our own families that Christmas wouldn't be Christmas without. Teresa's homemade eggnog has become a favorite holiday delicacy at the Byrd home.

Contrary to popular belief, however, you don't need to schedule large blocks of time to create delicious Christmas treats. And you don't have to be a culinary whiz to whip up delightful holiday dishes. We have included in this chapter recipes that the busiest people can make. Even the self-proclaimed worst cooks can tackle any of these festive foods without fear.

Children of all ages will enjoy helping, too. A two-year-old child will get a big kick out of stirring the batter and decorating the giant gingerbread man. With minimal adult supervision, an older child can cook many of these treats.

Family and friends alike will enjoy gifts of food your kids have made. So don your aprons and put on the old Bing Crosby "White Christmas" album. Great memories can be made in the kitchen!

**"The first thing I'm going to do. . . is. . . bake fruitcakes. . . . If no one eats them, we'll use them to extend the patio after Christmas."**

*Erma Bombeck*

## Cakes, Cookies and Crunchy Treats

**Christmas Yule Log**
1 package cake mix
1 16-ounce can chocolate frosting
Green maraschino cherries
Red hot candies

Preheat oven to 300⁰. Prepare your favorite cake mix according to package directions. Grease and flour two 1-pound coffee cans. Pour half the batter into each can. Bake cakes until a wooden pick inserted in the center comes out clean, about 50 to 55 minutes. Cool cakes in cans 5 minutes, then remove them from cans. Allow cakes to cool completely on a wire rack. Then slice off the uneven end of each cake.

On a pretty platter, place cakes end to end; glue them together with a layer of frosting. Frost the cake completely. Using the pointed tines of a fork, create bark-like marks on the frosting by dragging the fork along the length of the log in a wavy pattern. Cut green cherries in half. Make a holly design on top of the log by placing three halves together. Place three red hots in the center of the cherries for the berries. Cake serves 12.

### Gingerbread Giant

1 box (14.5 ounces) gingerbread mix
⅓ cup warm water
Raisins

Combine gingerbread mix with water, stirring until well mixed. Cover dough with plastic wrap, and refrigerate for 20 minutes.

Preheat oven to 350⁰. Grease a large cookie sheet. Remove dough from refrigerator, and pinch off a large piece for the body. Press it round and flat, and place it on the cookie sheet. Pinch off a slightly smaller piece of dough, shape it into the head, and attach it to the top of the body. Pinch off pieces for legs; roll them into round, flat shapes, and attach them to the body. Repeat the same procedure for the arms, using slightly smaller pieces.

Press raisins in the dough to make the eyes, nose and mouth, and put three raisins in a row down the middle of the body for buttons. Bake the cookie for 15 to 20 minutes or until light brown.

Let gingerbread cool 5 minutes on the pan. Remove cookie from the pan, and allow it to finish cooling on a wire rack.

### Kid-Proof Fudge

1⅓ cups sweetened condensed milk
3 cups chocolate chips
1½ teaspoons vanilla
½ cup chopped nuts
Pinch of salt

Butter an 8x8x1½-inch square pan. Cook sweetened condensed milk and chocolate chips in a 2-quart saucepan over medium heat, stirring constantly until the chocolate is melted. Remove pan from heat; add vanilla, nuts and salt, stirring mixture just until smooth. Spread fudge in the pan; cool it in the refrigerator 2 hours or until firm. Cut the fudge into 1-inch squares. Makes 64 candies.

### Christmas Lollipops

¼ cup margarine or butter
½ cup light corn syrup
¾ cup sugar
½ teaspoon vanilla
Food coloring
18 lollipop sticks (available at craft stores)

Spray a cookie sheet with nonstick vegetable coating. Place lollipop sticks 2 inches apart on a cookie sheet. Combine butter, corn syrup and sugar in a 2-quart pan. Bring mixture to a rolling boil, and continue until it reaches 270⁰ on a candy thermometer. Remove pan from the heat, and stir in vanilla and food coloring. Pour about 1 tablespoon of hot syrup on one end of each stick. Cool lollipops completely, about 30 minutes. Remove them from the cookie sheet. Store them in an airtight container, or wrap each lollipop with plastic wrap secured with transparent tape. Makes 18 candies.

### Chocolate-Peanut Butter Truffles

2 cups peanut butter
½ cup margarine or butter, softened
1 1-pound box powdered sugar
2 tablespoons shortening
1 12-ounce package chocolate chips

Mix peanut butter, margarine and powdered sugar. Shape mixture into 1-inch balls; refrigerate until firm. Heat shortening and chocolate chips over low heat, stirring constantly until chocolate is melted and mixture is smooth. Remove pan from heat. Dip balls one at a time into melted chocolate; place balls on a cookie sheet lined with waxed paper. Refrigerate candy until firm, about 30 minutes. Makes 3 dozen.

### Chocolate-Maple Balls

3 cups finely crushed vanilla wafers
1 cup finely chopped pecans
½ cup maple syrup
1 cup powdered sugar
½ cup cocoa powder
4 tablespoons light corn syrup
Powdered sugar or cocoa

Mix vanilla wafers, pecans, syrup, powdered sugar, cocoa powder and corn syrup, stirring until smooth. Shape mixture into ½-inch balls. Roll balls in powdered sugar or cocoa. Makes about 4 dozen candies.

### Quick Candy Mints

8 ounces white chocolate
1 cup crushed peppermint candy canes

Butter a rimmed cookie sheet. Place chocolate in the top of a double boiler over hot (not boiling) water. Heat until chocolate is melted, stirring occasionally. Stir in crushed peppermint candy. Spread mixture on the cookie sheet. Refrigerate 30 minutes. Break candy into pieces. Makes about 6 dozen candies.

### Crispy Christmas Trees

¼ cup margarine or butter
40 marshmallows
10 to 15 drops green food coloring
5 cups crispy rice cereal
Red hots
12 cone-shaped paper cups

Heat margarine and marshmallows in a 3-quart saucepan over low heat, stirring constantly until marshmallows are melted and mixture is smooth. Remove pan from heat; stir in green food coloring and rice cereal until well mixed. Press rice mixture into the cone-shaped paper cups. Refrigerate cups for 10 minutes. Tear cup away from cookie, and decorate each tree with red hots, pressing them into the sides and top. Makes 12 trees.

# Savory Seasonings and Treats for Gift Giving

### Glazed Spiced Nuts

1 tablespoon egg white
2 cups pecan or walnut halves
¼ cup sugar
1 tablespoon cinnamon

Preheat oven to 300°. Slightly beat egg white

in a medium bowl. Mix sugar and cinnamon with the egg white; add pecans or walnuts, stirring to coat nuts completely. Spread sugared nuts on an ungreased baking sheet, separating nuts to avoid clumps. Bake nuts for 20 minutes or until light brown. To give nuts as a gift, package in glass canning jars or Christmas tins.

### Herb Vinegar

1 quart white vinegar
1 clove garlic
1 medium piece fresh basil or 1 teaspoon dried basil
1 medium piece fresh dill or rosemary or 1 teaspoon dried dill or rosemary

Place vinegar, garlic, basil and dill or rosemary in a 2-quart, stainless steel (don't use aluminum) saucepan. Cook vinegar mixture over medium heat until it starts to simmer. Remove pan from heat, cover, and let it sit 1 hour. Strain vinegar mixture, and discard garlic and herbs. Pour vinegar into gift jars. Add 1 piece of fresh or 1 teaspoon dried dill or rosemary to each bottle; seal bottles with a cork or lid. Wrap a ribbon around the bottle or jar with a tag that gives instructions to use the vinegar in salad dressings. The vinegar is also nice for marinating beef or pork.

**Note**: Help your children make this vinegar and the following oil for teachers. Fresh herbs are usually available at grocery stores, but you can substitute dried herbs. Interesting jars can be found at container and craft stores.

### Herb Oil

4 cups olive or vegetable oil

3 or 4 pieces fresh basil, marjoram, rosemary or thyme, or a combination of these herbs
1 bay leaf

Place herbs in decorative bottles. Fill bottles with oil; seal with corks or lids. Let oil sit at least one week to allow the herbs to release their flavors. Package as you would the herbal vinegars. The oil is nice for salad dressings and marinades.

### Seasoned Salt

2 cups salt
1 teaspoon onion powder
1 teaspoon dry mustard
1 tablespoon paprika
1 tablespoon garlic powder
1 tablespoon finely crushed dried oregano

Mix all the ingredients together. Fill jars using a funnel; then seal jars with a cork or lid. Give bottles with a tag that says to use as with any seasoned salt. This salt is great on french fries, baked chicken and salads.

**Note**: Children five and older can stir this mixture together. Mom can help fill the jars if necessary. Empty spice jars can be saved and recycled, or new ones can be found at container and craft stores.

### Spiced Tea Bags

4 teaspoons crushed cinnamon sticks
1 teaspoon whole cloves
1 teaspoon grated nutmeg
4 teaspoons tea leaves (herbal or any other variety)
4 6-inch double layers of cheesecloth
Kitchen twine

Combine spices and tea leaves. In the center of each cheesecloth square, place a fourth of the tea mixture. Gather up the edges, and tie each square into a bag with the twine. Give the bags with instructions that each one will brew the same amount of tea as a commercial tea bag.

### Strawberry Butter

1 cup margarine or butter
1 10-ounce package sweetened, frozen strawberries, thawed
½ cup powdered sugar (or less to suit taste)

Place all ingredients in an electric mixer bowl, food processor or blender. Beat mixture until smooth and no lumps in the butter remain. Spoon butter into canning jars; seal with lids. Give instructions with the butter to use it on bread, crackers, pancakes or waffles. This butter keeps in the refrigerator for 2 weeks. It makes 2 cups.

# Food for Family Entertaining

### Teresa's Eggnog

2 cups sugar
1 quart half-and-half
8 eggs, separated
2 cups whole milk
1 quart whipping cream
Dash of salt
Freshly grated nutmeg

Combine sugar and half-and-half, stirring until sugar dissolves; set this aside. Whip cream. Beat egg yolks with electric mixer until thick and lemon colored. Gradually add whole milk, beat-ing constantly at low speed. Add half-and-half mixture gradually to egg yolk mixture, stirring well.

Beat egg whites until stiff peaks form. Gently fold egg whites into yolk mixture. Fold in whipped cream and salt. Refrigerate eggnog. Stir before serving. Sprinkle each serving with nutmeg. This eggnog tastes better the next day. Makes 1½ gallons.

### Cheese Ball

8 ounces cream cheese
4 ounces grated cheddar cheese
4 ounces crumbled Blue Cheese
1 tablespoon grated onion
1 tablespoon Worcestershire sauce
½ cup chopped pecans, walnuts or almonds

Combine softened cream cheese, cheddar cheese, blue cheese, grated onion and Worcestershire sauce, mixing with an electric mixer until smooth. Shape cheese mixture into a ball, then roll it in chopped nuts. Wrap the ball in plastic wrap, and refrigerate. For giving, wrap the ball in colored cellophane, then place on a disposable Christmas dish. To serve, place cheese ball in the center of a plate, and surround the ball with crackers.

### Banana Christmas Candles

4 lettuce leaves
2 bananas
4 slices canned pineapple
4 red maraschino cherry halves

Place the lettuce leaves on four salad plates. Put a pineapple slice in the center of each lettuce leaf. Peel the bananas, and cut them in half. Stand the flat end of each banana half in the middle of each pineapple slice for the candle. Cut off the tip of the banana, and place a cherry half on top for the flame. Salad serves 4.

### Christmas Vegetable Tree

1 12-inch Styrofoam cone
2 large bunches parsley
4 cups assorted fresh vegetables, such as cherry tomatoes, turnips, broccoli, cauliflower or carrots
**Herb Dip** (see recipe below)

Wash and dry parsley. Starting at the bottom of the cone, cover Styrofoam form with small bunches of parsley, leafy ends turned down. (You'll need about twenty large paper clips cut in half, or U-shaped pins or wire.) Secure parsley to the cone with U-shaped paper clips, overlapping each bunch to cover the clips. When you get to the top, turn the leafy ends up so they cover the tip of the cone; make sure no Styrofoam is showing.

To make vegetable shapes, slice turnips (unpeeled) into ½-inch slices. Using small cookie cutters, cut out such shapes as stars, angels or animals. A turnip star is especially cute at the top of the tree. Cut remaining vegetables into bite-size pieces.

Let children use toothpicks to attach the vegetable ornaments to the tree. Place the tree in the middle of a large serving tray, and surround it with snow (**Herb Dip**).

### Herb Dip

1 lemon

2 cups sour cream
2 cups mayonnaise
2 tablespoons grated onion
2 tablespoons crushed dill weed
Salt and black pepper to taste

Squeeze the lemon; mix the juice with the remaining ingredients. Cover dip; refrigerate 1 hour. Serve dip with fresh vegetables or crackers.

## Christmas Morning Breakfast or Brunch

### Festive Orange Drink

1 quart orange juice
½ cup maraschino cherry juice
Red and green maraschino cherries

Mix orange and cherry juices. Place red and green cherries alternately on toothpicks. Fill small glasses with ice and juice, and garnish with a cherry skewer.

### Cinnamon Pull-Apart Coffee Cake

3 cans Hungry Jack biscuits
1 cup margarine or butter
1½ cups brown sugar
2 teaspoons cinnamon
1 cup chopped pecans

Preheat oven to 300°. Grease a bundt pan with butter. Combine butter, brown sugar, cinnamon and pecans in a small saucepan. Heat on low, stirring often until butter is melted. Cut each can of biscuit dough into fourths. Put half the biscuit pieces in the pan. Pour half the butter mixture over the biscuit pieces. Layer with remaining biscuit pieces and butter mixture. Bake 45 minutes. Remove coffee cake from oven; let it sit in pan 5 minutes. Turn coffee cake onto serving plate. Serves 10.

### Christmas Brunch Bacon

1 pound thick-cut bacon
½ cup brown sugar
2 tablespoons yellow mustard

Preheat oven to 350⁰. Place bacon in a single layer on large rimmed baking sheet, making sure the pieces don't touch. Mix sugar and mustard together, then spoon it over bacon slices. Heat bacon in oven 10 to 15 minutes or until sugar is melted. Using a fork, remove bacon slices, leaving as much sugar as possible. Place slices on a serving platter in a single layer. Bacon will be very sticky and slightly crunchy. Serves 8 to 10.

### Bacon-Cheddar Quiche

4 eggs
¾ cup half-and-half
5 slices bacon
2 tablespoons Dijon mustard
2½ cups grated cheddar cheese
1 9-inch deep dish pie shell

Preheat oven to 350⁰. Cook bacon until crisp; then crumble it. Beat eggs lightly; then mix in the half-and-half, bacon, mustard and cheese. For a crustless quiche, pour the egg mixture into a buttered, 10-inch pie pan.

For a regular quiche, pour the egg mixture into an unbaked pie shell. Bake crustless quiche for 35 minutes or the regular quiche for 40 minutes.

# Chapter 12

# How to Give Away Your Christmas

Five-year-old James sat on the Peels' couch absorbed in one of the many Christmas catalogs that came in the day's mail.

"Mommy, Mommy, I want this and that, these and those! Please, Mommy, can I have all these things for Christmas?"

His childlike candor caused Kathy to smile and give him a big "We'll see about it" hug. She wondered, though, how she could shift his focus from receiving to the joy of giving in a way he could understand.

When we focus all our attention on what we hope to receive, we miss an important part of this season. The spirit of Christmas is upon us when we find ourselves in a generous mood stemming from a deep gratitude toward God. As parents, we can create an atmosphere that fosters a practical expression of gratefulness by helping our children get their minds off themselves and onto others.

**"Christmas is coming, the geese are getting fat, Please to put a penny in the old man's hat; If you haven't got a penny, a ha'penny will do, If you haven't got a ha'penny, God bless you!"**
*Beggar's Rhyme*

To begin a tradition of giving, your family may want to choose one of the suggested activities to specialize in each year. The following ideas can help you and your children give away your Christmas.

1. Take a basket of Christmas gifts to a family that's struggling financially. Include food, clothing and toys, as well as Christmas cards, stamps, transparent tape, ribbon and wrapping paper. Many churches and civic organizations have the names of families in need at Christmas.

2. Send Christmas cards, and write encouraging messages to military personnel on duty overseas. You can also bake and send Christmas goodies. Check with your local armed services office or newspaper for addresses and restrictions.

3. Pack a box of Christmas goodies, and take it to the firefighters on duty Christmas Eve. This is a family tradition at the Byrd home. Find out which station is in charge of protecting your home. Thank those people for being on duty Christmas Eve. Many times if they're not busy, they will let young children see the fire trucks and even try on a helmet. The police on duty Christmas Eve would enjoy some treats, too!

4. Bake cookies with your children for the mail carrier and sanitation workers. Have your kids watch for them so they can give them the cookies.

5. Offer to run errands for a homebound person. Let your children go with you to the person's home to find out what he or she might need. You can help the person buy presents or go to the post office or grocery store.

6. Go caroling as a family at a nursing home. Call beforehand to find out what restrictions apply and what time is best to go. Talk to young children before you go so they'll know how to respond to awkward situations that might occur. On one nursing home visit, the Peels' youngest son tried to give an orange to a lady in a wheelchair. James didn't understand why she let the orange roll right out of her lap. After learning the lady was blind, he placed the orange carefully into her hands.

7. Volunteer as a family to help at a soup kitchen for the homeless.

8. Write Christmas greetings with permanent markers on red and green helium balloons. Deliver them to patients in the hospital. Call the hospital before you go to get permission to visit. They can tell you the room numbers of patients who would enjoy receiving the balloons.

9. Let your kids make Christmas breads and goodies to give to baby-sitters, school bus drivers, teachers, Sunday school and music teachers and doctors and nurses.

10. Help an elderly neighbor or friend decorate his or her home for Christmas. A person never gets too old to enjoy pretty lights and decorations. Help him or her take down and store the decorations at the end of the season.

11. Invite a single parent and his or her children, a single person or an elderly couple over to share Christmas dinner with your family.

12. Obtain rolls of quarters from your bank. Keep the quarters handy so you'll always have money for your children to drop into the Salvation Army buckets when you're out shopping. You might even drive around just for the purpose of letting the kids look for the people ringing the bells beside the red buckets. (We use quarters because young children love hearing the money clang in the bucket.)

13. Give an anonymous gift of money to a needy family. Decide whom you would like to receive your gift. Buy a money order to mail to the family. Include a holiday message, but don't sign your name. One family we know even opened a special checking account and made arrangements with the bank to sign the checks in an unrecognizable way so they could give away money anonymously.

# Chapter 13

# 75 Ways to Celebrate Every Day

### "Until further notice, celebrate every day."

*Tim Hansel*

Our families are living in turbulent times. They need Home Sweet Home to be a shelter that offers rest, renewal and plenty of opportunities for recreation. A few years ago, the Peels decided their family motto would be "Life's too short not to have a good time." Families need to have fun together regularly, but it's easy to let days, weeks and even months slip by without making happy memories.

The smallest acts can create a fun atmosphere in our homes and turn an ordinary day into a celebration. The time we spend making even the most insignificant occasions special will be stored in our children's memory banks. The extra effort we make to show our love in a small way to our spouse may be the very thing that makes his or her day bearable.

During stressful times, we can help each other gain a positive and courageous outlook by purposefully looking for things to celebrate. One single mom told us she was struggling to support her family. To save money, she and her children stayed each night in the one room of their home they heated. Instead of complaining about their situation, however, they looked for a way to celebrate. That room became their adventure room, and they looked forward to doing something fun together every night.

Our children probably won't remember the thousands of chores we do for them or the many projects we're involved in. But we're convinced that our small attempts to make family life fun will turn into warm memories.

Holidays and special occasions compose only five percent of our living time. The remaining ninety-five percent is made up of ordinary days.[1] We've listed seventy-five ways you can orchestrate opportunities to help your family and friends celebrate life daily.

**Fun Things to Do for Kids**

1. Have a first-things party. Celebrate a young child's first bicycle ride without training wheels, first day of school or first tooth lost. It's also fun

to celebrate your child's first haircut. Be sure to take pictures, and save some hair clippings in a small envelope. Celebrate an older child's first day to drive a car, first date or first paycheck.

2. Begin a family fantasy file. Clip articles and advertisements with information about a vacation you'd like to take, or a car, computer or toy your kids dream of owning. Brainstorm about ways to earn and save extra money for these items.

3. Celebrate the day a child gets his or her braces off. When Judie's kids had theirs removed, she served some of the foods that had been on the off-limits list, such as corn on the cob.

4. Ask your child to make a list of his or her favorite five-minute, thirty-minute and two-hour activities that you can do together. The list can be as long as you desire. Keep this list handy, and try to do two or three of these things a week. Depending on the child's age, the list might include:

Five-minute activities: Throw a football. Sit together and read aloud from a favorite book. Have a tickle war. Play a duet together on the piano. Play a game of hopscotch on the sidewalk.

Thirty-minute activities: Take a walk around the block. Work a crossword puzzle. Rearrange the furniture in my bedroom. Play a board game. Plan a party.

Two-hour activities: Go to the park for a picnic. Build a model. Go to a batting range. Go shopping.

5. Celebrate your child's half-birthday. Bake half a birthday cake. First bake one round layer,

and then cut it in half. Stack the halves, and frost them as usual. For a present, give them a pint-size jar filled halfway with nickels and dimes to spend on a treat.

6. Make a young child feel special when baby brother or sister comes home from the hospital. Babies usually receive a lot of attention and presents, and it's easy for older siblings to feel left out. Go out for an ice cream or other treat, and buy the child a big-brother or big-sister present.

7. Help a daughter celebrate and make a keepsake of the first time she receives flowers. When the flowers wither, save the dried petals to make potpourri with a few drops of scented oil. She can put the flowers in a pretty bowl in her room.

8. Plan a surprise vacation to say, "Thanks for being such good kids." One mom told us she and her husband secretly saved their money and planned a trip to Walt Disney World for their daughters. They picked them up from school one day and drove straight to the airport. Talk about a surprise!

9. Buy your teenage daughter a hope chest. One family's tradition for generations has been to present each daughter with a hope chest on her thirteenth birthday. Add items periodically that your daughter will save for her own home.

**More Fun Family Activities**

10. Make a large Welcome Home banner for a family member who has been out of town. Place it in the front of your house to celebrate his or

her arrival.

11. On a cold winter day, celebrate the fun you had as a family on last summer's vacation. Get out vacation pictures. Talk about where you want to go next year.

12. Dress in costumes, and surprise Dad or Mom at the airport when he or she comes home from a business trip. If it's a lengthy trip, send letters to the hotel while the person is away.

13. Keep a basket handy for surprise picnics—just to celebrate a beautiful day.

14. Draw a warm bath for a family member who has had a stressful day. Warm and fluff his or her towel in the dryer.

15. Let your child help deliver helium balloons to Dad's or Mom's workplace to celebrate the closing of an important project or a promotion. This is also fun to do on a birthday or anniversary.

16. Send greeting cards or letters to your spouse and children when you're out of town. Before Kathy goes on a trip, she addresses letters and funny greeting cards to her family. She then asks a neighbor to mail them on designated days so that one arrives each day she's away.

17. Give a toast to different family members regularly. It can be as simple as holding up a glass of lemonade and saying, "To James, the best kickball player in kindergarten" or "To Dad, the best hamburger griller this side of the Mississippi."

18. Have a refreshing, old-fashi for a spouse or child who has be a difficult project or doing yard work ....ot day.

**Old-fashioned Soda**

3 tablespoons grenadine (cherry syrup) or chocolate syrup
1¼ cups chilled club soda or sparkling water
1 scoop of ice cream (vanilla or chocolate)

Mix grenadine or chocolate syrup and ½ cup of club soda or sparkling water in a 10-ounce glass. Add ice cream and remaining club soda. Stir immediately with a straw.

19. Kidnap a family member who has had a hard week, and take him or her to a favorite restaurant. Use a bandanna as a blindfold, and travel in a roundabout way to your destination. Have the person try to guess where you're going.

20. Hide an encouraging note for a family member in a surprising location. A drawer, shoe or frequently used cabinet is a good hiding place. Judie's son wrote a note to her and taped it inside the medicine cabinet. She appreciated this so much that she didn't want to remove the note. It's still there today.

21. Encourage Dad to make Saturday mornings special. One dad we know woke his boys up early on many Saturdays to go fishing or out to breakfast. They pretended they were sneaking out for a special men-only adventure they couldn't tell Mom about. (Of course, Mom had been secretly clued in to the plan.)

22. Teach a child to give a small present to

someone for no reason except to say, "I love you." Just realizing someone went to the trouble of buying your favorite pen or candy bar can make you feel loved. You can also schedule an afternoon with your child to bake cookies or make a present for a friend who is having a hard time. Deliver the gift together.

23. Buy a magazine or paperback book, and pack it in the suitcase for someone going on a trip. It's also fun to write affectionate notes and hide them in different locations in the suitcase of the traveling person. Bill does this for Kathy when she travels, and they do this for their boys when they go away to camp.

24. Show honor to your spouse or children by serving them breakfast in bed one Saturday morning. Include the morning paper for an adult or the comics for an older child.

25. Help new neighbors celebrate their new home. Take over a sack of easy-to-prepare foods. Include soft drinks, soups, sandwich supplies, chips and dessert. Don't forget paper plates and cups.

26. Celebrate the first fire in the fireplace this winter. Fix popcorn and cocoa, and sit by the hearth together.

27. Celebrate finishing a monumental household task, such as putting up a basketball pole and hoop. Fix the workers **Energy Juice.** Mix equal parts of lemonade and grape juice. This makes a delicious fruit drink.

28. Let your child celebrate your family pet's birthday or adoption day. Give your pet a special brushing or rubdown and a new chew toy.

29. Be alert for uncommon celebration days. For example, celebrate the anniversary of the first man on the moon (July 20, 1969).

30. Make World Series week a fun time at your house. Post scores and results on the refrigerator. Create a team banner, and put it on your front door. Keep peanuts and popcorn on hand, and serve hot dogs at least one night during the games. (This is also fun to do for other sports' play-off series.)

31. Cheer for green lights when you're in the car. The Byrd children made up a silly song, "Green light, green light, we love you!" They sang it every time Mom or Dad didn't have to stop at a red light. (Their college-age children still remember the song.)

32. Surprise your spouse or children by turning back their beds, fluffing up the pillows and leaving an interesting magazine. Place a small chocolate or treat on their pillow. They'll feel like royalty!

33. Make a monthly ritual as a family of delivering a small plant, fruit or cookies to a shut-in. Help this person celebrate an ordinary day. Be sure to call ahead to check on particular dietary restrictions and visiting hours.

34. Decorate the room of a sick or hospital-

ized family member with balloons, crepe paper and inspirational posters. Create a giant get-well card from poster board. Take it to the patient's school or office for friends to sign.

35. Have a family awards night. Invent crazy awards, and present award ribbons to each person. Possibilities include: Best Sport When Kidded. Best Closet Organizer. Best Plate Cleaner. Quickest to Answer the Phone.

**Fun Ways to Give Your Young Student a Lift**

36. Secretly fill a young person's car to the brim with balloons when he or she receives an honor at school or improves in a subject.

37. Let your students know how much you care by clipping articles of interest from the newspaper or magazines. Write a note in the margin that says you thought they might enjoy reading them. Slip the articles in their briefcase or backpack, or post them on the refrigerator door. Judie's kids are interested in animals and business. She routinely clips articles on those subjects for them.

38. Help a child who is involved in a big project at school. Do some of his or her regular chores. Start a family philosophy that says, "We all work together to help the person who is under the pile. Then we all celebrate together when it's over!"

39. Pack an extra-special sack lunch on the day of a difficult test. Send an extra treat to share with a friend.

40. On Wednesdays, celebrate the fact that the school week is half over.

41. Encourage a child who didn't win something and is feeling down. For example, recognize a child's creativity even though she didn't win the science fair competition. Or honor a son who didn't make the baseball team.

42. Surprise your child by going out to breakfast before an ordinary school day.

43. Create a "You Made It!" sign. Stick it in your front yard for a homesick child who stuck out a long week at camp. Keep a "Congratulations!" sign handy, too. Put it in the yard when your child scores points for his or her team or passes a big test.

44. Decorate your children's rooms with crepe paper and banners to congratulate them for giving their best effort on a book report or to praise them for being so diligent in a class they don't like.

45. Make a big deal out of the artwork and projects your child brings home from school. Display them on a special table or on windows, doors, cabinets or laundry room walls.

46. Pack a surprise afternoon snack for the kids in your car pool. Brian Byrd loved it when Judie brought a thermos of cold milk, small paper cups and brownies for the kids in their car pool.

47. Celebrate the end of each six weeks at school. Kathy decorates her kids' favorite cake with "Congratulations on a Great Six Weeks!"

The cake is waiting on the counter for them when they come home that day.

48. Celebrate the last day of school with young children. After school, take them to the dime store and give them one dollar to spend and twenty minutes to spend it in. You'll be surprised how much thought goes into the purchase.

49. Celebrate the end of summer and the start of a new school grade with your junior high or high school student. The Peels take a carload of kids to a water park each year for one last fling before school starts.

## Great Ways to Brighten a College Student's Day

"A survey shows that college students prefer ties with dots, suits with stripes, and letters with checks."[2]

Here are some fun and practical ways to remember your students:

50. Go out to dinner the night before your child goes away to college. One family we know made a family tradition of eating at a particular restaurant before each departure back to college.

51. Send your student an exam survival kit. Fill a shoe box with his or her favorite cookies, raisins, beef jerky, crackers, a mug and instant hot cocoa mix, highlighter pens, sticky-backed notes, legal tablets and other study supplies. It's also fun to send a package of balloons to brighten the dorm room, a Frisbee, a Nerf ball, stress vitamins and a bottle of aspirin.

52. Send funny greeting cards regularly. College kids need a little humor to relieve the stress of studying.

53. Make a "We Miss You!" poster with family snapshots for your student to hang on the dorm room wall.

54. Mail a box of laundry supplies, a roll of quarters and a couple of new magazines to read at the laundromat.

55. Put together a special midterm madness box just to say, "I love you." A daughter's could include dusting powder, perfumed soap, a new washcloth or sponge and other toilet articles. Boys always love to receive food and usually need soap, shaving supplies and cologne. Stick in a puzzle, art book or something else your young person is especially fond of.

56. Create a kitchenette kit. Send a plug-in pot to heat water, instant soup mixes, hot drink mixes, bouillon cubes, instant dinners that come in throwaway cups, dried fruits, cheese in push-button cans and crackers. (You'll need to check specific dorm regulations).

57. Mail a ten-dollar bill with instructions for your young person to eat a steak dinner at a local family steak restaurant.

58. Send a Dr. Mom's cold survival kit. Include aspirin, cold tablets, cough drops, throat lozenges, chicken bouillon cubes, vitamin C and a box of facial tissues.

59. Wire fresh flowers or a green plant to cheer up your student and his or her dorm room.

60. Create a sewing and repair kit for your student. The kit should include thread in various neutral colors, needles, straight pins, safety pins, quick glue, small scissors, a tape measure, iron-on patches, rubber bands and fusible webbing (to fix cuffs or hemlines).

61. Put together a correspondence kit to make it easy for your son or daughter to keep in touch with friends and relatives. Include postcards, stationery, greeting cards, pens and pencils, sealing wax, stamps and a small address book.

62. Check to see if someone who lives in the college area bakes and delivers cakes and goodies to college students. Call the college for a listing. This makes it easy for you to make sure your student has a birthday cake on his or her special day.

63. Send a sports survival kit. Pack head and wrist bands, athlete's foot powder, deodorant, energy bars, a sports magazine and golf or tennis balls or other items that correspond with your student's favorite sport.

64. Buy a small bulletin board for students to hang on the dorm room door. They can post messages when they leave the room about where they can be found and what time they plan to be back. A bulletin board also comes in handy when friends need to leave messages.

65. Mail a congratulations packet to a student who passes a big test or receives an honor. Include a congratulations banner (available at most party supply stores), confetti and enough snacks or treats so that other dorm friends can be a part of the celebration.

66. Pack a shoe-shine kit in a decorative tin for your son. Send brown and black shoe polish, two applicators, a brush, a couple of old rags (old pantyhose cut into rags work great), leather cleaner and new laces for athletic shoes.

67. Send a car-care box to your college student. Include a large sponge, two or three old towels or rags, glass cleaner, a roll of paper towels, a chamois cloth, an ice scraper, a new key chain and a whisk broom.

68. Subscribe to your son or daughter's favorite magazine, and have it delivered to his or her college mailbox.

69. Send a special message on a giant Colossal Gram® (nearly 5-by-7-foot) novelty telegram. You can order one by calling 1-800-222-GRAM.

70. Mail inexpensive cardboard door or room decorations for different holidays and seasons, such as shamrocks, hearts and patriotic figures. These are available at greeting card or dime stores.

71. Send a Christmas basket at the end of November. Include a Christmas music cassette or CD, a small Christmas candle (if allowed), a small artificial Christmas tree and ornaments, a greenery garland to hang above the door, an Advent calendar, a five-dollar bill tied with a rib-

bon (for little extras), a string of lights for the dorm window, Christmas cards, stamps and a new red pen.

A single son or daughter or college student living in an apartment will appreciate receiving many of the above items and special packages. Here are some additional things you can do for him or her:

72. When you go to visit your young adult, cook casseroles that freeze well, and stock his or her freezer. Judie tries to do this regularly for her daughter who lives in another state. She also takes easy-to-prepare foods for the pantry, healthy snacks and vitamins. Many times young people in college or a new job don't have time to cook healthy meals for themselves.

73. Send a spring cleaning survival box filled with cleansers, dish towels, a roll of paper towels, rubber gloves, a new dish brush and sponge.

74. Make cuttings from your potted plants for your son or daughter to start. Philodendrons root easily in water. You might also take some small pots and potting soil.

75. Keep a box easily accessible in your laundry room or garage to store duplicate household items that you find you don't need and can share with your son or daughter. Take the box the next time you visit, or mail the box when it's full.

1. Alexandra Stoddard, *Living a Beautiful Life* (New York: Random House, 1986), 4.
2. E.C. McKenzie, *14,000 Quips & Quotes for Writers & Speakers* (New York: Grenwich House, 1980), 92.

# Chapter 14

# Celebrating on a Shoestring

Fun isn't something we buy but something we make ourselves. Great memories can be created without a fat bank account. The fun quotient of the events we plan has more to do with our attitude than with the cost, location and accoutrements. Some of our best memories were made when times were lean.

If we wait until we can afford to celebrate, chances are we never will. When their children were young, the Byrds lived in a quaint but small house. Hardly a week went by when some kind of party or event for kids, neighborhood or church wasn't held at their home. They regularly had wall-to-wall people. A slim bank account didn't stop them from hosting fun events regularly. Their kids still have fond memories of those times.

They have since moved to a larger house and still practice the same open-house policy. Judie teaches classes for young mothers who want to know how to provide a hospitable atmosphere in their own homes while on a tight budget.

## "That man is the richest whose pleasures are the cheapest."

*Henry David Thoreau*

Another mom we know raised nine children. She baked a cake every school day while her kids were living at home. It was an inexpensive after-school snack for nine hungry kids and their friends. On Friday nights, her kids also knew they could each invite a friend over, because Dad always cooked more than enough hamburgers on the grill. Although they weren't wealthy, they bought cake flour and ground beef in bulk and practiced creative hospitality.

Don't let opportunities to celebrate slip by because you think you can't afford to make an occasion special. Celebrating can be surprisingly inexpensive.

1. Plan ahead. Write down all the items you'll need for the occasion. Give yourself enough time to watch for specials. For example, if you're hosting a party for teenagers in August, buy the canned drinks right before the Fourth of July,

when drinks usually go on sale.

2. Start a loose change jar. The Peels saved all their small change for a year in a gallon jar. When Bill received his postgraduate degree, they had saved enough money to buy graduation invitations and have friends over for a dinner party.

3. Decorate with fresh flowers and greenery. Let your kids plant flower seeds in your yard or in pots inside your home to keep fresh flowers always blooming. They can arrange them in vases or tall glasses. In the winter, use small evergreen branches and baskets of pinecones they've gathered.

4. Buy a case of pint-size canning jars. Use them for party glasses. With a lemon sliver attached to the rim, they make adorable lemonade glasses.

5. Let your children help build a family dining room table. Begin with a 4-by-4-foot piece of interior plywood. Scribe a 4-foot diameter circle on the plywood, using a pencil and string secured to the center point of the board with a thumb tack. Parents should carefully cut off the corners with a jig saw; children can help sand rough edges. Place this round form on top of an ordinary card table. Use a sheet or pretty fabric to make a round tablecloth that extends to the floor, covering the underside of your table. Your table will seat six or seven people. The Peels still use their first homemade table when they have family parties and need to seat a lot of people.

6. Dress up an ordinary table by making 12-inch square cloth napkins from pretty fabric or sheets. Bandannas also make colorful napkins. They can be washed and used over and over.

7. Create colorful tablecloths. Cut fabric at least 10 inches wider than your table, and 10 to 15 inches longer than your table. For example, use denim for a hamburger cookout or pink cotton fabric covered with lace netting for a luncheon.

8. Make pretty, tie-dyed paper napkins. Accordion-fold a large paper napkin or paper towel so it looks like a fan. Then fold the napkin in half lengthwise. Hold the middle of the napkin securely with a clothespin. In a shallow bowl, mix ½ cup water with 8 drops of food coloring. Dip ¼ inch of all four corners of the napkin into the colored water. Carefully open the napkin and allow it to dry completely. After it dries, refold it as a napkin.

9. Give a gift of personal coupons. Instead of buying a present, write down different ways you will serve the honoree. For example, a parent can give a child redeemable coupons for fixing a favorite dessert, fifteen minutes of nonstop wrestling, ten minutes of pitching the baseball, an hour on Saturday morning to repair a doll house or take a trip to the park.

A child can give a parent a coupon for a garage clean-out, a car wash or fifteen minutes of any chore the parent chooses. Give an adult friend a day of free baby-sitting for her birthday. Agree on a date you will do the service when you give the coupon so the recipient will know you are serious.

10. Buy an inexpensive potted plant. Wrap the plastic planter with sheet moss (available at most craft stores or nurseries), and secure it with a hot glue gun. Tie raffia around the moss-covered pot. This makes a lovely gift, and it will look like the creation of a professional florist.

11. Ask the produce manager at your grocery store for empty mushroom, berry or Belgian lettuce boxes. These are really cute lined with colorful tissue paper and make nice containers for gifts, potted plants or craft projects.

12. Ask interior designers and furniture stores for their out-of-date fabric samples and books that they would ordinarily throw away. Use the fabric samples to make napkins, table runners and to line baskets. It's also fun to wrap a present in fabric and tie it with grosgrain ribbon.

13. Dress up and be your own singing telegram to a family member or friend.

14. Organize a party for families at a city park. Play old-fashioned games like leap frog, relay races, softball and red rover. Take a big thermos of lemonade and sacks full of popcorn that you've popped ahead of time. Popcorn is inexpensive and can be fixed in lots of interesting ways.

### Ranch-Style Popcorn
1 (1-ounce) envelope ranch-style salad dressing mix
¾ cup vegetable oil
4 quarts popped popcorn

Sprinkle dry salad dressing mix over popped corn in a large bowl. Drizzle oil over popcorn mixture, stirring well. Allow popcorn to sit 2 hours, stirring occasionally. Store popcorn in an airtight container. Yield: 16 cups.

### Pizza Popcorn
¼ cup grated Parmesan cheese
2 teaspoons Italian herb seasoning
2 teaspoons salt
1 teaspoon paprika
1 teaspoon garlic powder
4 quarts popped corn

Combine the Parmesan cheese, herb seasoning, salt, paprika and garlic powder in a large bowl. Stir in popped corn; toss with the seasoning until it's evenly coated. Store popcorn in an airtight container. Yield: 16 cups.

### Caramel Popcorn
2 cups margarine
2 cups brown sugar
1 teaspoon salt
1 teaspoon vanilla
1 teaspoon soda
6 quarts popped corn

Boil margarine, sugar and salt for 5 minutes in a medium saucepan, without stirring. Add vanilla and soda, and gently shake the pan to mix. (Stirring will cause crystals to form.) Pour syrup over corn, and stir to coat it. Bake popcorn at 200° for 1 hour, stirring mixture every 15 to 20 minutes. Yield: 24 cups

15. Host a potluck dinner. Ask each family to be responsible for one part of the dinner. That way, one family doesn't carry the entire burden

for the meal. A progressive dinner is also fun. Eat each course of the meal at a different family's home. This is also a fun activity to organize for your church youth group or a school club.

16. Get together with several families whose children are similar in age to yours, and buy outfield or end zone tickets for baseball or football games. Take your own snacks, since stadium food is usually expensive. One group of young families did this regularly and became known as the end-zone gang.

17. Plan a parents-kids trade-out time with another family. Let one couple plan activities for all the kids for a Friday night and Saturday. It's their responsibility to take care of the kids for that time while the other set of parents spends the time alone—something all couples need periodically. Plan another weekend to switch roles. Single parents can do this, too.

# Chapter 15

# Creating the Best Birthday Party Ever

It's funny how our perspective changes drastically as we grow older. Birthdays can't get here fast enough for young children but come too fast for their parents! Even so, birthday celebrations are precious moments in life—whether it's a boy's sixth birthday, Dad's over-the-hill fortieth or Grandma's seventy-fifth.

Even birthday catastrophes can become funny family memories we can enjoy year after year. Judie's children remind her annually about the time she broke her foot on the day of Brian's sixteenth birthday party. She had to get her cast put on quickly before 100 kids arrived for a backyard cookout. And Kathy's kids tease her without mercy about baking birthday cakes that resemble the Leaning Tower of Pisa!

Depending on our circumstances, we all have a different capacity for pulling off birthday celebrations. If you're a single mom or dad trying to balance a full-time job while raising three

**"A mother bakes her child's birthday cake big enough to hold all the candles and her own small enough not to."**

children, you may need to pick up a cake at the grocery store and let the pizza parlor do the work for your child's birthday.

You'll find that the rewards outweigh any time and trouble you spend to celebrate a family member's birthday on a large or small scale. We all appreciate having our own special day remembered.

To help make those celebrations special, we've included My Own Party Planner for kids and Parents' Checklist in one chart on page 112. The kids' planner offers places to list ideas for food, decorations, party favors and games.

Make copies of the chart for your kids to use as a guide for their own parties. They'll have fun searching for ideas not only in this chapter but throughout *Holiday Survival*.

Use the following party ideas to spur your thinking. Don't feel you have orchestrate a huge production. You may only want to try one or two ideas for a small party.

# Fun Party Ideas for Younger Children

1. **Circus Party.**

a. Ask each guest to come dressed as a clown.

b. Create a mini-midway in your backyard, setting up some of the following events for the children to try. Give small prizes, such as trinkets and candies, to every child regardless of performance.

c. Cover empty 16-ounce cans with colorful contact paper. Stack them in pyramid formation, and let the children try to knock them down with tennis balls.

d. Paint a lake scene on a refrigerator or furniture box. Cut a hole high enough on the box so the kids can't see inside and large enough so they can stick a small fishing pole into it. Make fishing poles by tying a 3-foot length of string to a 3-foot dowel rod or stick; attach a clip-type clothespin on the end of the string. Have someone hide inside the box and put small prizes on the clothespin when the children go fishing in the box.

e. Write the names of small, inexpensive prizes, such as plastic animals, play watches, airplanes and jewelry, on slips of paper. Insert the paper slips into balloons (one per balloon); then blow up the balloons and tie them with a 6-inch length of string. Staple the strings to a fence or a large box that you've painted to look like a fence. Let the kids throw darts at the balloons. When a balloon pops, the child gets the prize stated on the slip of paper. (Be sure you have adult supervision for this activity.)

f. Set an assortment of wide-mouthed, empty jars on a small table. Have the children stand 3 to 6 feet from the table and try to toss pennies into the jars. Award a prize when three pennies land in the jars. Adjust the distance based on a child's age and ability.

g. Create a clown portrait screen. Paint a life-size clown without a face on a refrigerator box. Cut a hole where the face should be. Let the children stand behind the screen and put their faces through the hole. Take their pictures.

h. Set up a table where the children can draw funny clown faces on balloons with markers. Use rubber bands to attach the balloons to chopsticks; let the kids take their balloons home.

i. Make balloon sculptures. Purchase long, thin balloons that clowns use to form animal shapes. Blow up the balloons for the children, and let them twist them around to make sculptures. You'll be surprised at the creative shapes they come up with! Award prizes for the most original, silliest and largest. Have enough award categories so that each child wins something.

j. Fill a large, plastic leaf bag with blown-up balloons. Have the birthday boy or girl sit on a special birthday throne; then let Mom or Dad dump the balloons on the child. (This was a special request from Brian Byrd for his fifth birthday party.)

k. Make clown cones. Place a scoop of ice cream on a tray lined with waxed paper. Put a pointed sugar cone on top of the ice cream for the hat, and place the cones in the freezer to harden. Make faces on the ice cream with frosting tubes or small candies such as red hots, gum drops or licorice strips.

2. **Pets on Parade Party.**

a. Cut out animal paw footprints (e.g., dog, cat or bird) from brown construction paper. Tape them to your front walkway, making a path to your door.

b. Create a doghouse tunnel from a large box; place it right inside your front door. Have each child crawl through it to enter the party. When the child reaches the end of the tunnel, have a plate of dog-bone-shaped cookies to sample. Use your favorite gingerbread cookie recipe to make the bones.

c. Ask each guest to bring his or her favorite stuffed animal. Before the party, obtain medium-size packing or produce boxes from a grocery store—one for each child. Have an adult cut strips of cardboard from the opposite sides of each box to resemble the bars on an animal cage. Let them decorate their boxes with colored markers as cages for their stuffed animals.

d. Fill a glass bowl with Goldfish crackers. Let each child guess how many crackers are in the bowl. Give a prize to the child whose guess is closest to the correct number.

e. Paint animal faces on the kids' faces with antiglare face blackener (used by athletes and available at grocery or athletic supply stores). Paint on whiskers, spots, black noses and lines to make animal facial expressions.

f. Have a Dog Catcher's race. Divide the children into two teams. At the starting signal, one child from each team must run on all fours to a designated spot and place a toy bone in a box; then the child runs back and tags the next runner. The losing team must roll over and play dead.

g. Play Monkey Shines. Cut out eight to ten 5-inch circles from one side of a refrigerator box. Paint a jungle scene on the box. Have an older child or adult hide inside the box and shine a flashlight through the various holes, 5 to 10 seconds at a time. Have the children try to throw bean bags through the hole where the light is shining.

h. Play Pin the Tail on the Rabbit. Draw a rabbit without a tail on poster board. Make rabbit tails from cotton balls. Instead of pins, use masking tape rolled into a circle, sticky side out. Put a circle of tape on one side of the cotton ball. Blindfold the children one at a time, and let them try to stick their tail on the rabbit in the appropriate place. Give a prize to the one who gets the closest.

i. Have the kids make surprise, glowing-cat party favors. Supply a 3-by-4-inch or larger yellow cellulose sponge (the kind that has large, irregular holes) and a 5-inch square of black felt for each guest. Have each person cut out a 3- to 4-inch circle from the sponge for the cat's head;

then cut pieces of black felt to make the ears, eyes, nose and mouth. Glue the face pieces to the sponge with a low temperature glue gun. Draw whiskers on the face with a black marker. What's the surprise? Place a flashlight behind the cat's face, and watch it glow in the dark!

j. Create silly snakes. Wrap a 12-inch pipe cleaner around a pencil to make a corkscrew shape. Remove the pencil. Shape one end of the pipe cleaner into a small circle for the snake's head. Glue on sequins for eyes.

k. Have a Dog Bone Treasure Hunt. Twist brown paper lunch sacks at each end; using brown package string or raffia, tie the bag two inches from each end to make a bone shape. Make one for each child. Before the children arrive, hide the bones in your yard. When you're ready to start the game, ask the children to pretend to be dogs and hunt for a bone. When they find a bone, they should stand beside the bone and bark. When all the children have found a bone and are barking, they can bring in their bones and trade them for a prize.

l. Create a cat cake. Bake and frost a round cake. Use round chocolate wafer cookies for ears; round red candies for eyes; a brown chocolate candy for the nose; black licorice strings for whiskers; a red licorice string for a smiling mouth. For party favors, send a box of animal crackers home with each child.

### 3. **Fun at the Beach Party.**
a. Turn your backyard into a pretend beach. Play water games and build sand castles. Fill two plastic wading pools, one with water and one with sand. (Sand is available at building supply stores.)

b. Put lots of pennies at the bottom of the pool filled with water. Blindfold the participants; let them see how many pennies they can pick up with one hand in thirty seconds. Give the winner a prize.

c. Hide small, plastic trinkets and toys in the sand. Set a time limit, and let the children hunt for the treasures using only one hand. At the end of the game, supply small bags for the children to take home their treasures.

d. Have a water balloon war. (Fill balloons with water before the guests arrive).

e. Have crazy bubbles for the kids to play with. Put 1 quart of water in a shallow tub; stir in ½ cup of sugar until it dissolves. Add five to six long squirts liquid dishwashing detergent, stirring again. Dip in various homemade bubble wands, using slotted kitchen spoons, funnels or plastic flyswatters with holes.

f. Buy inexpensive, plastic sun visors at a craft store. Let the children decorate the visors with acrylic paint pens.

g. Serve sandwiches and cookies in plastic pails. Sit on beach towels to eat. Let the children take their pails home as party favors.

### 4. **Space Travel Party.**
a. Create a spaceship in your dining room. Cover the table with aluminum foil. Hang silver

curling-ribbon streamers from the ceiling or light fixture. Blow up lots of silver or white balloons, and attach them to chairs, ceiling and door frames. Hang a few shooting stars from the ceiling, using cardboard stars covered with aluminum foil. Hang the stars with thread and straight pins.

b. Give each guest a 12-by-14-inch piece of poster board. Supply buttons, markers, scraps of fabric and glue for them to create rocket instrument panels.

c. Make a time capsule for future earth travelers. In a metal box, place several small objects, along with a short message each child has written. Put a sign on the box that reads: To Be Opened in the Year _____. (You decide the year.) Bury the box. Put a marker on the spot so the birthday child can find it the year it's to be opened.

d. Give rocket favors. Cover empty toilet-paper rolls with foil, enclosing one end. Fill each one with candy and small treats. Decorate cone-shaped paper cups; glue each one on top of a rocket. Set the rockets in a cluster in the middle of the table for the centerpiece until the party is over.

e. Serve astronaut space food. Put refreshments in self-sealing plastic bags. Even punch—Tang, of course!—can be served in a bag. Fill the bag half full, and zip it up. To drink the punch, open the bag just enough to slip in a straw.

f. Make apple robots. Use a yellow or green apple for the robot. Break toothpicks in half, using them to attach large marshmallows on each side of the apple to look like ears. For the face, attach two blueberries for eyes and a strawberry for the nose. Cut a maraschino cherry into the shape of a smile for the mouth. Place a round slice of orange (¼-inch thick) on top of the apple, securing it with a toothpick to resemble a hat. Cut about 1 inch off the end of an unpeeled banana, and place it on top of the orange slice. Place the apple robot on a lettuce leaf to serve. Children will love removing and eating each part of the robot. (Make sure small children do not eat the toothpicks.)

g. Put sparklers on the birthday cake instead of candles.

5. **Artfest Party**
a. Cover a table with a solid-color bed sheet. (Be sure to put a protective layer of plastic or newspaper over the table first.) Use permanent markers to write the birthday child's name and age in the middle of the sheet. Let each guest draw a picture and sign his or her name. Later you can use this sheet to make an indoor play tent.

b. Create a decorative, party-favor sack. Cut triangles around the top of an ordinary lunch sack to look like the tips of crayons. Make each point a different color using markers. Use the sack to carry the art projects the kids made and to give a small box of crayons, markers or other art supplies the kids used.

c. Make wallpaper beads. Cut colorful wallpaper into 1-inch circles. Cover the back of each circle with white school glue. Starting at one side, roll each circle into a cylinder around a pencil, leaving a small opening in the middle of the cylinder. Quickly slip the wallpaper bead off the pencil so it doesn't stick, and let the bead dry. String the beads onto dental floss, fishing line or thin yarn to make a necklace.

d. Design costume masks from egg cartons. Cut out two adjoining egg-holder cups. Cut a circle out of the center bottom of each cup for eye holes. Punch holes in each side of the cups; insert a pipe cleaner in each hole. Bend the pipe cleaners to fit over the child's ears. Decorate the masks with glitter, felt, markers or feathers.

e. Make a balloon paddle game. Decorate a paper plate with markers. Punch a small hole in the center of the plate with the point of a pencil. Thread 2 inches of a 36-inch piece of kite string through the hole, and tape or staple the string to the back of the plate. Next use a cool-type glue gun to attach a wooden paint stick to the back of the paper plate and on top of the string. Tie the neck of a blown-up balloon to the loose end of the string. See how many times you can paddle the balloon up into the air without stopping.

f. Create yarn bracelets. Draw a line 1 inch from the top edge of a Styrofoam cup. Cut around the cup on the line to make a bracelet. Wrap pretty yarn around the Styrofoam form, covering it completely. Glue the end of the yarn to the inside of the bracelet. (Check at your local craft store for interesting types of yarn.)

g. Bake giant sugar cookies; let the children decorate their own with tubes of frosting and sprinkles.

# Great Party Ideas for Older Children

6. **I.Q. Party**

a. Ask guests to come to the party dressed like nerds. Give a prize for the best costume.

b. Set up board games for the kids to play, such as Checkers, Parcheesi, Tile Rummy and Trivial Pursuit.

c. Provide number puzzles and brain teasers for the kids to play and solve as teams. A good resource book is *Solve It!* by James F. Fixx. The team with the most right answers wins a prize.

d. Play Categories. Give each player a sheet of paper with the alphabet listed in a row down the left-hand side. Choose a subject, then ask the players to write words that relate to the subject beside the appropriate letter. The player who writes the most words wins.

e. Play Affinity. Divide the kids into two teams. Set a timer for ten minutes, and see which team can list the most items or words that go together (e.g., bigger and better, hit and run, black and blue).

f. Go on a Nerd Scavenger Hunt in your neighborhood, or have adults drive the kids around to the homes of friends to ask for items on the list. You might include a plastic pocket protector, old white sock, a sheet of college-ruled paper, a leaky ballpoint pen, an ugly tie, a pair of broken glasses and a hair net.

g. Have this party at night so you can go to the park and play Sardines. Ask one player to volunteer to be "it." All the players except this one cover their eyes. The person who is it hides. Then everyone hunts for the hidden person. As each player finds the hidden person, that player hides there, too, until all the players are packed into the hiding place—like sardines! The last person left becomes it for the next game. (For safety, set boundaries on where the children may hide.)

h. Serve nerd food, such as bologna sandwiches, dill pickles and sardines and crackers. (You'll probably want to have some foods kids like on hand, too.) Use individual Hostess Twinkies for birthday cakes.

### 7. Come as a Famous Person Party

a. Ask kids to come dressed as a famous person.

b. Cut out stars from construction paper; tape them on the walkway to your front door.

c. Hang a large, foil-covered star on your front door. As each guest arrives, take his or her picture by the star. Make a big deal of his or her arrival. Announce the famous person in a flashy way.

d. Before the party, secretly ask the parents of each guest to loan you a baby picture of their child. Display those pictures in your house. After the party starts, have the kids try to guess the name of the baby in the picture. Ask them to write down their guess; award a prize to the person who has the most correct answers.

e. Play familiar songs, asking volunteers to take turns doing lip syncs of the songs. Use a serving spoon for a pretend microphone. Vote on the best performance. (If you offer a good prize, you'll get more participants!) Make a video of this event; then play it back for the stars to see themselves on TV.

f. Make Hollywood sundaes. Provide three or four different flavors of ice cream. Offer the following toppings: chocolate and caramel syrup, fruit sauces, various kinds of crumbled cookies and candy bars, an assortment of nuts and raisins, whipped cream and cherries for the top.

### 8. Sports Party

a. Decorate your home with team pennants, sports posters, balloons and crepe-paper streamers.

b. Play baseball with a whiffle ball or touch football with a foam rubber football.

c. Hold track and field events. For example, have a broad jump, a 25-yard dash or a jump rope contest. You can also see who can stand on one foot the longest or keep a ball or balloon bouncing in the air the longest. Award prizes to the winners.

d. Have a Popcorn Relay. Divide the kids into two teams. For each team, put a glass soda pop bottle in a large bowl (to catch the dropped kernels) on a table. Between the bowls set another large bowl filled with unpopped popcorn and two scoops. Have each team line up in front of a bowl. Starting with the first person in line, each member of the team tries to get as much popcorn into the bottle as possible with one scoop of kernels. After the scoop is emptied, the player passes the scoop to the next player to try. The first team to fill the bottle wins. The losers run a lap around the backyard!

e. Watch the thirty-minute video "Take Me Out of the Ball Game," a *McGee and Me* video available at Christian bookstores.

f. Give packages of baseball cards and bubble gum for favors.

g. Serve popcorn, peanuts and hot dogs.

h. Make the following fun birthday cake.

### Popcorn Birthday Cake

1 cup sugar
⅓ cup light corn syrup
⅓ cup water
4 quarts buttered popcorn
Gumdrops and other candies for decorations

Mix sugar, corn syrup and water in a medium saucepan; boil mixture until it reaches the light-thread stage (230⁰) on a candy thermometer. Remove pan from heat. Place buttered popcorn in a large glass or metal bowl; pour hot syrup over the popcorn, and stir until it's evenly coated. Grease a large angel food cake pan with mar-

garine; then pack the popcorn into the cake pan. Let the popcorn set for 1 hour until completely cool. Insert a wet knife around the edges of the popcorn cake to loosen it from the pan. Invert the cake on a serving plate.

If desired, decorate the cake with gumdrops or other candies. To serve, cut the cake with a serrated knife.

9. **This Is Your Life Party**

a. Make this a surprise party for a teenager. Before the party, make a videotape, interviewing the birthday child's friends. Ask each friend to give a birthday greeting and a short message about his or her friendship with your child. Play this tape at the party.

b. You can also send a letter and a self-addressed, stamped envelope to the friends, asking them to write a birthday greeting for your child and send it back to you secretly. Collect the messages, and present them to your child at the party. They will be treasured always.

c. Create a centerpiece for your dining room table with your child's framed photos, baby cup, a favorite old stuffed animal, awards and memorabilia. You can also make streamers from several colors of curling ribbon. Hang the curled ribbons from the light fixture over the dining room table. Tie small balloons to the ends of several streamers to create a festive look.

d. Make a birthday album with pictures from birth until the present day to give to the one being honored at the party. Write funny captions under the pictures.

e. Buy a light-colored, decorative pillow. Ask each guest to autograph the pillow with an indelible colored marker.

f. Let the guests help preserve this occasion. Capture the honoree, and wrap him or her head to toe in toilet paper. Take a picture of the mummy and friends.

g. Serve your child's favorite foods for the party meal and dessert.

**Birthday Invitation Ideas**

10. Blow up a balloon. Write party information on the balloon, then deflate it. Place the balloon and some confetti inside an envelope with the following riddle:

"You must blow,
  If you want to know.
When will it be?
  You will see!"

11. Glue small toy mirrors to poster board cut into invitation-size squares. Write "Look who's coming to the party!" under the mirror, along with the party information.

12. Make a secret message invitation. Write out the party information on construction paper. Cut the paper into simple puzzle shapes, and put the pieces in an envelope. The receiver must put the puzzle together to learn details of the party.

13. Write your party message in a circle. Begin in the middle, and follow a spiraling path. Make photocopies of your finished circle invitation, and send them to friends on the guest list.

14. Write a slumber party invitation on a colorful paper tote-style gift bag. Include instructions to use the bag to bring a toothbrush, night clothes and other needed items.

15. Make a paper scroll. Cut white paper the length of two lollipop sticks, and write the party information on the paper. Glue the sticks to the side ends of the paper, and roll it up. Secure the scroll with a ribbon tied in a bow.

16. Write a poem about your party for the invitation. For example:
On Friday, March 1, Clint Smith will turn six;
we've invited a clown to perform magic tricks!
We hope you'll come from three until four,
to 515 Fifth Street—just knock on the door.

# My Own Party Planner

**Name:** Trey

**Event:** Birthday Party     **Date:** Sept. 4

What kind of party do I want to have? List choices:

1. Sports Party ✓
2. Famous Person Party
3. Roller Skating

Where do I want to have the party? List choices:

1. Backyard ✓
2. Lincoln Park
3. Skating Rink

Friends I want to invite:

| | |
|---|---|
| Jennifer | Peggy |
| John Peter | Craig |
| Amber | George |
| Caleb | Brian |
| Molly | |
| Kelly | |

Food:

Page numbers in *Holiday Survival:* 5, 28, 94

| | |
|---|---|
| Ice Cream Cake | |
| Mt Saint Helen's Dip | |
| Energy Juice | |
| | |

Decoration and party favor ideas:

Page numbers in *Holiday Survival:* 109

| | |
|---|---|
| Sports posters | Pennants |
| Blue and yellow balloons | |
| | |

Activities, crafts and/or games:

Page numbers in *Holiday Survival:* 108, 109, 110

| | |
|---|---|
| Popcorn relay | |
| Track and field events | |
| Balloon paddle games | |

## Parents' Checklist

☑ Confirm date: Sept. 4

☑ Set time: 3:00 p.m.

☑ Reserve place: backyard

_____

☐ Send invitations: by Aug. 30

**Food to make:**

☐ Ice Cream Cake

☐ Mt. Saint Helen's Dip

☐ Energy juice

☐ _____

☐ _____

**Decorations & party favors to buy or make:**

☐ Baseball cards

☐ Bubble gum for prizes

☐ Balloons

☐ _____

**Games & activities to set up:**

☐ Popcorn relay

☐ Wiffle ball

☐ Sack race

☐ _____

☐ _____

☐ _____

**Shopping list**

☐ Popcorn

☐ Lemonade

☐ Grape juice

☐ Candles

☐ Cake mix

☐ Ice Cream

☐ Chocolate syrup

☐ Gum

☐ Balloons

# My Own Party Planner

| | |
|---|---|
| **Name:** _____ | **Parents' Checklist** |
| **Event:** _____ **Date:** _____ | ☐ Confirm date: _____ |
| What kind of party do I want to have? List choices: | ☐ Set time:_____ |
| 1. _____ | ☐ Reserve place:_____ |
| 2. _____ | _____ |
| 3. _____ | ☐ Send invitations:_____ |
| Where do I want to have the party? List choices: | Food to make: |
| 1. _____ | ☐ _____ |
| 2. _____ | ☐ _____ |
| 3. _____ | ☐ _____ |
| Friends I want to invite: | ☐ _____ |
| _____  _____ | ☐ _____ |
| _____  _____ | Decorations & party favors |
| _____  _____ | to buy or make: |
| _____  _____ | ☐ _____ |
| _____  _____ | ☐ _____ |
| _____  _____ | ☐ _____ |
| _____  _____ | ☐ _____ |
| Food: | Games & activities to set up: |
| Page numbers in *Holiday Survival:* _____ | ☐ _____ |
| _____  _____ | ☐ _____ |
| _____  _____ | ☐ _____ |
| _____  _____ | ☐ _____ |
| _____  _____ | ☐ _____ |
| Decoration and party favor ideas: | ☐ _____ |
| Page numbers in *Holiday Survival:* _____ | Shopping list |
| _____  _____ | ☐ _____ |
| _____  _____ | ☐ _____ |
| _____  _____ | ☐ _____ |
| _____  _____ | ☐ _____ |
| Activities, crafts and/or games: | ☐ _____ |
| Page numbers in *Holiday Survival:* _____ | ☐ _____ |
| _____  _____ | ☐ _____ |
| _____  _____ | ☐ _____ |
| _____  _____ | ☐ _____ |

# Chapter 16

# Family Ties: Planning a Great Reunion

"Mom, did you really try to drive that old Chevy at your uncle's house when you were twelve years old? I'll bet your seat was sore for days when you got caught!"

At family reunions, our children learn a lot about their heritage, plus a few interesting facts about our own childhoods we were hoping would remain secret. They can gather quite a bit of information to use against us if they listen closely to the "Remember when . . ." tales told by assorted aunts, uncles and cousins.

Family reunions also stir up a strong sense of family pride within us. When extended families get together, traditions are passed from generation to generation. Grandparents and parents enjoy telling stories and reliving the past. This strengthens family ties and helps to instill a love of family in the children, even though they're usually too busy enjoying their long-lost cousins to realize something significant is taking place.

As the years pass by quickly, it's easy to lose

**"Nothing creates a firmer belief in heredity than cute, well-mannered kids at a family reunion."**

touch with family members. The adventure of planning a family reunion, whether a yearly tradition or one planned out of the blue for the first time, can really be fun.

The following tips will help you simplify the project so you can enjoy the reunion, too.

1. Ask another family member to share the responsibilities. This will lighten the load and double the fun. It's a good idea to start planning a year in advance.

2. Set a date. Call several family members who are especially interested in a reunion, and settle on a date that fits the most schedules. You'll never find a date that's best for everyone.

3. Research possible locations. Call or write for information and guidelines at city parks, state parks, recreational clubs or lakes. If you're a sports-minded family, choose a place where you

can put up a volleyball net or have a tug-of-war.

4. Send a letter of information to each family, including the date, location and other pertinent information. You'll also need to calculate how much money each family needs to contribute for expenses so they can plan on this ahead of time.

5. Mail a biographical questionnaire to each family. Also ask for a recent family picture. The pictures and information can be photocopied and compiled into a booklet that will help different branches of the family tree get to know each other at the reunion.

6. Make assignments for food. An old-fashioned potluck meal works well. Various family members can be in charge of bringing beverages, meat dishes, salads, desserts and paper goods.

It's also fun to have each family member bring a box lunch in a foil-lined corsage or shoe box. Tell people to be sure to list the contents of the lunch on the outside of the box. The lunches can be traded or auctioned off to help defray the cost of the reunion.

7. Divide entire extended family into set-up and cleanup teams beforehand. You may also want to assign the positions of official photographer, video camera operator, children's activities coordinator, song leader, adult recreation director, transportation and accommodations coordinator and family historian.

8. Send a confirmation letter two weeks before the reunion with important information and last-minute details.

9. Make name tags for all those who will be attending, or have supplies ready for families to design their own tags when they first arrive at the reunion. If families will be divided up for sports events or activities, you can color-code the tags to signify teams. Or encourage each family to make creative name tags ahead of time that will help others remember their name. For example, the Bakers could make a small paper chef's hat with their name written across the front of the hat. The McDonalds could make tags using Scottish plaid ribbon.

**Family Reunion Activities**

10. Start your reunion off with a crowd mixer game to help extended family members get to know each other. Before the reunion, write the names of every family member vertically down the left side of a piece of paper. Make copies of this list, and hand them out as people arrive. (Be sure to have a good supply of pencils available.) Ask people to find as many people on the list as possible within a certain time limit. When they identify someone, they must ask that person one of the following questions and record the answer by his or her name:

a. What's your favorite hobby or activity?

b. Where did you go on your last vacation?

c. What's the most interesting thing that happened to you during the past year?

At the end of the time limit, the person with the most answers wins a new scrapbook.

11. Family tree: Ask an artistic family member to bring a painting of a large tree. (The blank side of a flattened refrigerator box works well.) Spend

time at the reunion filling in the branches with family names.

12. Crazy hat contest: Encourage each family member to bring a crazy hat. Set aside a time for everyone to model their hats. Vote and give funny prizes to the winners of these categories: cutest, most unique, largest, most practical and ugliest.

13. Design a special family T-shirt that commemorates this event. Collect shirt sizes beforehand; have a T-shirt shop print your family name and logo or special design on the front. Have family members wear their T-shirts at the reunion.

14. Honor grandparents and senior members of the family. Ask them to talk about the biggest change in the world during their lifetime, the first house they lived in and the happiest memory of their childhood.

15. Family olympics: Divide your extended family into teams. The following events are fun: a three-legged race; an egg toss; croquet, badminton or table tennis tournaments. Award crazy prizes to the winners.

16. Personalized plastic glasses: Buy colorful, inexpensive, plastic tea glasses at a discount store. Personalize the cups before the reunion, using permanent paint pens. For example, you could put: "Smith Family Reunion—1993." Family members can use the cups at the meals and then take them home as reunion souvenirs.

17. Family journal: Ask a family member with writing skills to collect interesting family facts and historical information during the reunion. Print a family journal or newspaper to commemorate your reunion, and send one to each family. You can also compile a family cookbook.

18. Play Who Am I? Ask each attendee to write on an index card an interesting fact or feat about himself or herself that few other family members know. The cards should not be signed. Collect the cards; have someone read each fact or feat aloud. Let the others guess who wrote it.

19. Set up an area where children can work on simple crafts and play games.

20. Have a family talent show by asking each family to come prepared with an act. You can also create a family band; ask musical family members to bring their instruments.

21. Ask all family members to bring old family photos and albums. This is a wonderful way of reliving family history.

22. Have older family members bring vintage clothing and give a style show.

23. Ask senior family members to bring pictures of old cars. Check in your area to see if it's possible to rent an old car for part of a day. If it is, give short rides to everyone.

24. At the end of the reunion, give funny family awards for the following: least hair, longest nap, worst sunburn and queen of potato salad.

# Chapter 17

# Are We There Yet?

Traveling over the holidays can bring out the worst in everyone. Usually Dad and Mom are stressed out from working up to the last minute. Then Mom plays her annual martyr role because she had to do all the planning and packing and she thinks she's the only one who never gets a holiday. By the time the family pulls out of the driveway, the kids are bouncing all over the car and asking, "How much longer till we get there?"

**"The intensity of your child's need to use the rest room on a trip is in direct proportion to the distance you must travel to find one."**

holiday travel tips to help make your trip a positive experience.

1. Prepare for your trip well ahead of time. Otherwise, you're liable to end up frazzled and in a bad mood. If possible, Mom and Dad should share the many errands required before a trip, such as picking up tickets, packing, servicing the car and making arrangements with neighbors to feed the pets and get the mail.

After several stressful holiday trips, our families have learned some serious lessons about traveling. Your journal entries about being cooped up in a car for eight hours or waiting in an airport all afternoon do not have to read like a Tennessee Williams play, where everyone comes home depressed and exhausted.

Many of the hassles that come with holiday travel can be avoided. Drawing from our victories and defeats, we've come up with the following

2. Pack your sense of humor, and enjoy the trip. Whether you fly your family to Europe or scrunch six people into a five-passenger car for an overnight campout at the state park, a positive attitude will help you survive bad weather, rude people, poor service and a host of other inconveniences. On one trip, the Peels allowed a pizza parlor with poor service and high prices to ruin their attitudes for an entire day. They decided their holiday time was too valuable to let that ever happen again.

3. Share the responsibilities of being driver and kids' referee. Interstate traffic may be a delightful change for one parent, while the other might have a fresh supply of patience for dealing with the kids in the backseat. When both parents are tired or a backseat catastrophe occurs, that's a good time to stop for ice cream, air out the car and change the seating arrangement. Then play a great tape you've been saving for an hour of desperation.

4. Decide on the agenda for your trip beforehand. Many husbands and wives have completely different ideas of what a trip should entail. Do you want a highly scheduled lineup of activities or a relaxed, hang-loose kind of holiday? The Peels confess to major marital conflicts several years running as they crossed the Continental Divide. Talking through their unspoken expectations before the trip helped them omit this annual battle from their holiday. Your kids will also have more fun if they can have a part in the planning.

5. Keep a notebook to rate the best and worst restaurants, hotels or motels, nice picnic spots and clean rest-room locations. You don't want to make the same mistake twice.

6. Leave phone numbers with a neighbor where you can be reached in case there's an emergency at your house while you're traveling.

7. Write down important information in an easily accessible location for Grandma or a baby-sitter when you and your husband go alone on a trip. You'll also need to leave a medical release form for each child in case of an emergency.

**Fun Things to Do While Traveling**

8. Play Look for the License Plates. Make a photocopy of a United States map from an atlas. Glue the map to a piece of cardboard, and cover it with clear contact paper. Every time a license plate from a different state is spotted, color in the state with an erasable marker. When you arrive at your destination, count the number of states you marked. Wipe off the board and play the game again on your way home.

9. Help a young child understand how long a trip will take. Before you leave, label two sandwich-size, self-sealing plastic bags with an indelible marker. On one write Bag A, and on the other write Bag B. Then place two peanuts in Bag A for every hour you think the trip will take. For instance, if you anticipate the trip will last six hours, put twelve peanuts in the bag. Every time thirty minutes pass, take a peanut from Bag A and put it in Bag B. At the end of the trip, all the peanuts will be in Bag B. Younger children love this game, and it helps them conceptualize the passing of time.

10. Let your child pack a travel box with small toys, art supplies, cassette tapes and other treasures. Add a couple new toys for surprise treats. A sturdy cardboard shirt box or a 13x9x2-inch metal cake pan with a metal lid will double as a storage box and lap desk in the car.

11. Take along joke and brainteaser books. They come in handy if you have to wait to get your car repaired. They're also fun to read together while waiting in an airport or for your food to be served in a restaurant.

12. Collect all kinds of coins on your trip. Start the collection with your child's birth year. Help younger children read the dates on coins each time you stop and receive change. Save those coins in an envelope. Older children will enjoy writing down all the birth years of family members, anniversary dates and interesting historical dates from the past twenty to thirty years. Have a contest to see who can find the coins with those dates first.

13. Play Boink. To play this counting game, one person starts by saying "one." The next person says "two," and so on. Every time a multiple of five comes up in numerical order, that player says "boink." The boink number can be changed to multiples of three, seven or other numbers to make the game more difficult. This is a great game for elementary-age children who are learning their multiplication tables.

14. Play Cucumber. One player thinks of an action verb. The other players ask questions to try to guess the verb. They must substitute the word *cucumber* for the verb until they guess the answer. For example: Do you cucumber every day? Do you cucumber in the morning? Do you cucumber your teeth? You *brush* your teeth! Warning: This game tends to make the players silly!

15. Older kids and adults will enjoy playing License Plate Lingo. The license plates of many states include letters as well as numbers. As you drive down the highway, jot down ten sets of the first letter combinations you see. For example, if the license plate reads WNR 241, you would write down the letters WNR. The object of the game is to think of words that contain those letters in the order presented on the plate. A possible solution for WNR could be *winter*.

16. Have each family member write a postcard telling about your trip. Include interesting sights you've seen, what you've done and where you've eaten. Address and mail the postcard to your address. It's fun to receive the cards when you arrive back home. Save the postcards each year in a special box.

17. Make pretend binoculars for a small child to sightsee with; tape two toilet tissue rolls together, side by side.

18. Play How Many? When you cross a state or county line, give each passenger a list of items to count as you travel. If your trip is short, begin your game when you start driving. You can count rivers crossed, service stations, American flags and parks. See who counts the most of each item at the end of the day.

**Air Travel Tips**

19. When you purchase your tickets, ask to be seated in the bulkhead seats, where there's more room for children to move around. If you buy tickets at the last minute, try to arrive at the airport early. Ask the flight attendant to arrange for you to sit with your children if your tickets don't designate that you're together. The airlines are usually very accommodating.

20. Call your travel agent or airline to arrange for special foods that children enjoy. Many airlines will provide a hamburger or sandwich for

a child instead of the regular adult meal.

21. Play Count the People while waiting in a terminal. You can count all the people wearing hats, all the bald-headed men or all the people with babies.

22. Ask the flight attendant if your child can meet the pilot. Many airlines are happy to let you do this and will even give your child a pilot's wings pin.

23. Bring along extra cans of fruit juice and snacks. If the plane is crowded, the flight attendants may not be able to serve you right when your child is cranky or hungry.

24. Pack gallon-size, self-locking plastic bags for dirty diapers.

25. Let each child take small toys and games in a backpack. If you must walk to another gate to change planes, the child can carry his or her own belongings.

26. Pack good reading, activity and coloring books to help pass the time.

27. Take a portable personal cassette player, earphones and tapes your child will enjoy. Check your local library and bookstores for good children's stories on tape. Elementary-age children will enjoy the "Adventures in Odyssey" series produced by Focus on the Family.

# Chapter 18

# A Weekend Vacation at Home

**"One nice thing about going home is that you don't have to make a reservation."**

It's Friday. Dad has just come home from a fast-paced business trip. Mom has finished a week of being swamped with job, community and family responsibilities. The kids look glazed-over after being carted every which way to ball practices, music lessons, tutors, youth groups and birthday parties.

The family hasn't spent much time together lately, and opportunities to have fun have slipped by unnoticed. But getting away for a weekend holiday is the last thing the family wants to or can afford to do.

Yet the schedule is so hectic, the family feels like throwing up its hands and saying: "Stop everything! We need some time to regroup and relax."

When that happens in your home, we suggest you turn an ordinary weekend into a holiday at home. The time your family spends cocooning can be a refreshing change from your busy schedule. We think you'll be raring to go again on Monday morning after a fun weekend together.

**Holiday at Home Plan**

1. Choose a date at least four weeks in advance. Advise all family members of the plan so that other engagements won't be accepted.

2. Mom and Dad need to do some advance preparations, such as buying the essential groceries for the weekend, getting the board games down from the closet to check for missing pieces and taking a trip to the video store to rent a good family movie.

We suggest you do not take the kids to the video store with you. Then you won't have to say no to some of the movies they may want to rent, and you avoid starting the weekend on a negative note.

3. Encourage Dad to leave work early and surprise the kids by picking them up at school. Ask him to stop at the grocery store and give each child a small amount of money to choose special snacks for the weekend.

4. Turn off your phone. Make a rule that no phone calls are to be made except for emergencies. You may want to leave your answering machine on. Let the kids record a fun message that explains to callers what you're doing.

5. Make a sign, and hang it on your front door so the neighbors will know what you're doing. Tell them your kids would love to play *after* your family vacation.

6. Start Friday evening with a fun dinner. If your kids are like ours, there's only one choice— pizza! Whatever you serve, don't eat in the kitchen or dining room. Spread a quilt on the floor, or eat outside. Do something out of the ordinary, and don't worry about manners tonight.

7. Decide beforehand what chores will need to be done even though you're on vacation. Try to keep them to a minimum. Rotate cooking and cleanup responsibilities.

8. Play games after dinner. If young children are present, be sure to play something simple so they can participate. When the young ones fall asleep, you can get out more-advanced games. Buy small prizes beforehand for the winners of each game.

9. At an appropriate time, start winding down the evening. Have everyone get into his or her pajamas and spread out sleeping bags or quilts on the family room floor. Pop some popcorn, and watch the family video. The night owls of the family can record who falls asleep first and who snores the loudest!

10. Have juice prepared for the Saturday morning early birds. When everyone finally wakes up, have a relaxed breakfast together. Make a rule that everyone must stay in pajamas and robes until at least ten that morning.

11. Plan a fun late-morning outing, such as visiting the zoo, browsing at a museum or puttering around antique or junk stores. It would also be fun to schedule a surprise adventure, such as a half-day trip fishing or ice skating, visiting a dairy farm or picking berries. Make sure it's something the kids will enjoy.

12. Schedule in free time. Everyone needs some space and time alone. Have good books, magazines, puzzles, models and the newspaper on hand.

13. Let the kids fix lunch. Be patient, and help them as needed. Have ingredients available for a simple meal: lunch meat and cheese sandwiches or hot dogs. Be sure to lavish a lot of praise on the kids for their efforts.

14. If weather permits, do something else active Saturday afternoon. Take a walk, go on a bike hike or throw a Frisbee at the park. If you can't go outside, put on lively music and take turns leading family calisthenics indoors.

15. Serve an easy meal on Saturday night, such as hamburgers or the following stew.

**Vacation-Day Stew**

2 pounds stew meat

2 chopped potatoes

5 chopped carrots

½ cup chopped celery
1 cup frozen peas
1 chopped onion
1 can cream of mushroom soup
½ cup water
2 or 3 bay leaves
Salt and pepper to taste

Combine the above ingredients in a covered casserole dish. Bake the stew at 250⁰ for 5 hours. Remove the bay leaves when the dish is done.

16. For dessert, let the kids fix **Chocolate-Chip Souffle.** One cookie at a time, dip an 18-ounce package of chocolate chip cookies in milk, layering them in a glass baking dish. Cover the soggy cookies with whipped cream or nondairy whipped topping. Serve immediately, or refrigerate until ready to serve.

17. Saturday night can be a fun time for wrestling matches, board games and family hide-and-seek. Turn out all the lights in the house, and play with flashlights. Let small children stick with Mom or Dad so they won't get scared.

18. After Sunday morning breakfast, attend church together. Go out to lunch after church, and talk about the fun things that have happened over the weekend. When you come back home, your vacation will be over.

# Chapter 19

# Expecting Unexpected Guests

How many times have you smiled through gritted teeth when your long lost aunt and uncle arrive unexpectedly at your front door with their six kids? Of course, they were just passing through on their tour of eleven southern states!

Or, worse yet, your preschooler expresses her creativity in every room of the house the day your husband surprises you and drops by with the boss. Or your high school son tells you after school that he invited the defensive line from his football team over for dinner tonight. And they weigh over 200 pounds each and don't eat quiche!

We want our kids to know their friends are welcome in our homes, and we want surprise company to feel welcome, too. After getting caught unprepared one too many times, we have come up with an emergency plan of action that goes into effect when unexpected guests arrive. Just having a plan helps us relax and enjoy the company without worrying about how the house looks or what we can offer our guests to eat.

## "Happy is the house that shelters a friend."

*Ralph Waldo Emerson*

When we don't appear to be rattled by their surprise visit, guests, including the ones our kids bring home, feel more welcome.

The following ideas will help you rise to the occasion when you're caught off guard.

1. If you see unexpected company walking up the front sidewalk, grab a laundry basket and pick up as much clutter as you can in thirty seconds. Sometimes it helps to just clear a path. Hide the basket in a closet; then put the things in their proper place when company leaves.

2. Keep a lipstick, compact, small hair brush and a tiny bottle of perfume in the kitchen so you can freshen up if someone arrives unexpectedly or the bathroom is tied up.

3. Have room sprays, scented light bulb rings or regular or simmering potpourri on hand to give your house a fresh scent in a hurry.

4. Stock an easy-to-tote bucket with glass cleaner, furniture polish, bathroom cleansers, rubber gloves and rags so you can do a quick surface cleanup.

5. Grow herbs such as summer or winter savory or scented geraniums in small pots on your window sills. On short notice, you can snip a few sprigs and arrange them in small vases to place around your house.

6. Create a colorful centerpiece for an unexpected occasion. Spray fruits and vegetables with nonstick cooking oil, polishing them with a paper towel. Snip sprigs from a green shrub or ivy; wash and dry them. Tuck them between the fruits and vegetables that you've arranged in a big bowl or on a platter.

7. Prepare a small basket of activities and toys for young children. Include a new coloring or activity book and crayons, plus a small car or action figure. Keep the basket up on the closet shelf. Save it for when you need to carry on an adult conversation and you would like something quick to occupy the kids. As your children grow older, save some of their toys in a box for younger guests to play with.

8. Order maps and information about local entertainment and places of interest from your Chamber of Commerce to have available for out-of-town guests.

9. Work out a plan with your family ahead of time about where unexpected overnight guests will sleep. If a child gives up his or her room for your company, be sure to show sincere appreciation.

10. Keep extra pillows and blankets to make quick pallets for the kids when guests arrive. Judie keeps a pile of quilts folded on a shelf in her family room. Her kids know they are welcome to invite friends over to spend the night.

11. Create a guest basket to have on hand. Fill it with items your guests might need but forgot to bring, such as a disposable razor, travel-size containers of aspirin, antacids, deodorant, hand lotion, shampoo, shaving cream, toothpaste and toothbrush (many times kids forget to pack theirs). Include a fresh bar of guest soap, small paper cups, and nice washcloths and hand and bath towels for guests only. Keep the basket in a place where it is easy to pull out.

12. Keep disposable diapers and a jar or two of baby food on hand for unexpected guests who have babies.

13. Pack a travel survival kit for out-of-town house guests when they leave. Include snacks, small cans of fruit juice, gum, mints and napkins. They will also appreciate a small toy or craft project for their children to play with on the way home.

14. Have colorful paper napkins, cups and plates on hand, just in case there aren't any clean dishes when friends arrive.

15. Post a list on the refrigerator door with locations of food, snacks and beverages that your

guests are welcome to eat.

### Easy Foods to Fix for Surprise Guests

16. Be prepared to serve a spur-of-the-moment hors d'oeuvre. Keep an 8-ounce package of cream cheese in your refrigerator and a box of interesting crackers hidden. (We have to hide them at our houses to ensure their preservation.) Place the brick of cream cheese on a pretty plate. Then pour a small jar of strawberry jam, jalapeño jelly or fruit chutney over the top of the cream cheese. (Chutney is located on the condiments aisle of the grocery store.) Surround the cheese with crackers.

17. Keep soda pop or fruit drinks to serve guests in a place that is off-limits to the kids. Let the kids have their own special place for their beverages. Keep both places well stocked.

18. Have the ingredients for an easy punch on hand. Mix 1 can of Hi-C fruit drink with 1 liter of lemon-lime soda.

19. Keep a frozen pound cake, ice cream and paper doilies on hand. Put the cake on a doily and pretty plate to turn an ordinary snack into a fancy presentation. Serve the cake plain or in bowls with ice cream. You can also add ice cream toppings and chopped nuts.

20. Make ordinary store cookies look elegant in a moment's notice by arranging them on a pretty plate covered with a glass cake dome.

21. Store individual portions of homemade chili in self-sealing plastic bags in the freezer for surprise dinner guests. Stick the chili in the microwave. And keep grated cheese and a bag of corn chips to serve with the chili. Both of these items freeze well.

22. Keep a **Pizza Roll** in your freezer for company.

### Pizza Roll

1 loaf frozen bread dough
½ cup Italian marinara or spaghetti sauce
¼ pound pepperoni, thinly sliced
½ cup grated mozzarella cheese
¼ cup sliced black olives
1 egg yolk

Preheat oven to 350⁰. Allow bread dough to thaw. Roll out the dough into a large rectangle about 16-by-16 inches on a floured surface. Spread the sauce over the rolled-out dough.

Place a row of pepperoni about 1 inch from the edge of one end of the rectangle. Fold that end of the dough over the pepperoni slices, flattening it with your fingers. Sprinkle cheese along the edge of the dough you just folded over. Fold the dough again to cover the cheese. Repeat this process using olives. Seal the ends of the roll and place it on a cookie sheet, sealed side down. Slightly beat the egg yolk with 1 teaspoon water; then brush the top of the dough with this mixture. Bake the pizza roll for 20 minutes until barely brown. Cool the roll, wrap it in foil, and freeze it. When unexpected guests arrive, pull the roll out of the freezer, and allow it to thaw for 30 minutes. Bake at 350⁰ for 30 minutes or until golden brown.

**Note:** Your kids will enjoy serving this to their friends.

**Guest Tips for Kids When They Visit Others**

Use the following suggestions to teach your kids how to earn the "Good House Guest Seal of Approval" when they stay at someone else's home:

23. Reply to invitations promptly.

24. Make sure your children arrive on time, or have them call if they're going to be late.

25. Teach your children to show interest in others. At a party, they can look for someone who might be alone and help him or her feel a part of the occasion.

26. Leave on time. If the kids must leave early, have them let the host and/or hostess know ahead of time. Tell them to slip out unobtrusively so they won't disturb the others.

27. Have the kids take a small gift of appreciation for more than an ordinary overnight visit.

28. Teach your kids to offer to help with the dishes, keep their belongings picked up and put wet towels in the laundry room when they leave.

They can ask the hostess if she would like them to take the sheets off the bed.

29. Before leaving, tell your children to give their host and/or hostess a sincere thank you.

30. If it was a lengthy visit or an out-of-town stay, have your kids send a note to say thanks. Judie wrote a generic thank-you for her kids to use as a guide until they learned how to write notes on their own.

31. Here's a sample thank-you note to use:

Date

Dear (name),

Thank you for all the fun things you did for me when I came to visit you. I especially enjoyed (list something you really liked doing). Thank you for (name something that was done for you, such a special bed made for you or a food or treat you liked). I hope to see you again very soon.

Love, or

Sincerely yours, or

Your friend,

# Chapter 20

# Saving the Memories

**"I'd save them in a treasure box,
Or jar with lid so tight;
Our family celebrations
Made life just seem so right."**

Special occasions and holidays can not only be enjoyed at the moment of their occurrence, but also ten, twenty, even fifty years later. It's a privilege to live in an age when we can look at the slides of our daughter's first birthday party on the eve of her wedding. When we get together to compare family reunion pictures from years past, we're reminded of the natural rhythm of life, who has been added to the family and who has passed away.

Both our families believe in taking lots of photographs. Our children love to look at photo albums and laugh at how Mom and Dad looked when they were first married. They never fail to comment, "Look! Dad had hair back then."

The kids also like to see how they've grown over the years, the places they visited and the friends they played with. David Byrd and John Peel have been friends since they were three years old. They laugh when they see the pictures Judie took of them painting the side of her house with

water when they were little. She also has endearing photos of the clubhouse Brian and his friends built from scrap lumber in her backyard. Those photographs are priceless souvenirs of fun times.

Old pictures of our ancestors are considered treasures. We've had many restored. They're displayed in almost every room of the house, giving us all a sense of belonging. It also reminds us of the importance and responsibility of passing down a godly heritage through our family line.

Because of advanced technology, we have almost limitless opportunities to save special family moments and events. The following ideas will give you some easy and practical ways to capture those memories and preserve your own family's history.

1. Keep your camera in an accessible location; always keep plenty of film on hand. Take your

camera regularly on family outings. Take funny candid shots at home. Our kids love to look at the pictures we snatched of them studying or asleep on the couch.

2. Have a professional family photo made every year. In the years to come, you'll be glad you did. This is one way to underscore the importance of family in a child's mind. Watch your newspaper for sales. Many studios run specials during the year. You can also ask a friend to take a picture of your family yearly with your own camera. A park is usually a nice setting.

3. Put together family photo albums. Write humorous captions for the pictures. One family we know keeps stacks of photos sitting around in attractive baskets for easy access. They label and date the back of the pictures. When their kids come home from college, they love to browse through those baskets.

4. Display lots of pictures of your children around the house. That will make them feel significant. Kathy has been collecting frames for twenty years. At last count she had almost 140 photographs of family and friends displayed all over her house.

5. Have a giant jigsaw puzzle made from a family photograph. Check with your local camera shop or film processing store.

6. Take videos of family events and outings. If you don't own a video camera, many video stores rent them.

7. Create a family press box. Save the newspaper on the day your children are born. They'll treasure it later.

8. Save clippings and articles from city newspapers, school newspapers or magazines that mention a family member's name. Some are fun to frame and hang in your home. The Peels are glad their ancestors started this tradition. They framed the front page of a 1930 newspaper with a picture and article about Bill's great-grandfather that has been passed down through the family.

9. Preserve a recent newspaper article for 100 years. Stir one Milk of Magnesia tablet with one quart club soda until the tablet is completely dissolved. Let the newspaper clipping soak for five hours. Remove the clipping, and soak it in plain water for one hour. Then blot excess water off the clipping with paper towels. Allow it to dry completely before storing it.

10. Keep a journal for each of your children. Record special things you've done together and memorable events. When your children say something funny or worth remembering, write it down. Keep cards and letters they've written to you. Give the journal to the child on his or her eighteenth birthday.

11. Create a memory box for each of your children. A plastic sweater box works well. Save a few school papers from each year, award ribbons, recital programs, a lock of hair from the first haircut, hospital bracelets, baby booties and other memorabilia.

12. Decorate a small jewelry-size box to save the tooth fairy's treasures. Baby teeth are precious possessions to young children. They love to get out their baby teeth periodically and count how many they have lost.

13. Save your son's first pair of cowboy boots or your daughter's favorite Easter dress. They can be framed in a shadow box when the child is grown. Judie saved her boys' boots for them, and Kathy loves having her six-year-old organdy Easter dress that her mother saved for her.

14. Make an audio-cassette birthday recording for each child every year. Talk about some of the ways he or she has grown, some humorous things that happened and how much he or she means to your family. Have the child record his or her own thoughts, too.

15. Help your children start and keep a school-year journal. When they are high-school seniors, they will be amazed at what they wrote when they were in first grade. Every year when school ends, have them fill in the blanks to the following questions:

a. Teacher's name
b. Favorite subject
c. Hardest subject
d. Best friend
e. Favorite food
f. Food I dislike the most
g. Favorite song, movie and/or book
h. Favorite sport
i. Favorite piece of clothing or outfit
j. Most embarrassing moment
k. News-making event

16. Create a family-traditions book for a son or daughter who is about to be married. Write what you do on holidays and special occasions. Tell about favorite family hobbies, foods, mealtime rituals and jokes. Describe fun activities you enjoy, places you like to go to, where you like to go on vacations and what you like to do. Present the book to your son or daughter on his or her wedding day. It will help the newlyweds get to know each other better.

17. Save the flowers from your daughter's wedding. Let them dry out; then make a wreath for her new home with the dried flowers.

## References

Chase, William D., *Chase's Annual Events: Special Days, Weeks & Months in 1989.* 1989. Chicago: Contemporary Books.

Goldblatt, Joe Jeff, *Special Events: The Art and Science of Celebration.* 1990. New York: Van Nostrand Reinhold.

Hatch, Jane M., *The American Book of Days.* 1978. New York: H. W. Wilson Co.

*The World Book Encyclopedia.* 1959. Chicago: Field Enterprises Educational Corporation.

Wright, John W., ed. *The Universal Almanac 1990.* 1989. Kansas City: Andrews & McMeel.

Dear Moms and Dads:

We hope you'll have as much fun using this book as we've had writing it. This project has been for us a celebration of the family, the home and the privilege of living in a country where we have the freedom to celebrate.

Please feel free to share your own family celebrations and holidays with us. If you'd like to be on our mailing list, we'd love to hear from you!

Write to Kathy Peel at:
P. O. Box 5100
Tyler, Texas 75712

Write to Judie Byrd at:
P. O. Box 573
Fort Worth, Texas 76101

The Peels: (from left) John, Joel, Bill, Kathy and James.

The Byrds: (from left) Brian, Teresa, David, Judie and Bill.

Kathy Peel co-authored the best-selling books *A Mother's Manual for Summer Survival* and *A Mother's Manual for Schoolday Survival* with Joy Mahaffey. She has been featured on "Good Morning America," "The Home Show," and in *Entrepreneur Magazine.* Her articles have appeared in *Family Circle.* She speaks frequently at conferences and conventions, and she has been married for 20 years.

Judie Byrd is president of Food and Entertaining. She has taught cooking and hospitality seminars to women's groups and corporations for more than 14 years. Her classes have been recommended by *Woman's Day* and featured in numerous newspapers as well as on cable television. Her articles have appeared in *Family Circle.* She has been married for 26 years.